INSIGHT CO

KV-638-305

# RIO DE Janeiro

GREAT LITTLE GUIDES

*Compact Guide: Rio de Janeiro* is the ultimate quick-reference guide to this pulsating city. It tells you all you need to know about Rio's attractions, from the delights of the Botanical Gardens to the heights of Sugar Loaf and Corcovado, from the sands of Copacabana and Ipanema to the rhythms of *Bossa nova* and Samba.

This is one of 120 Compact Guides, which combine the interests and enthusiasms of two of the world's best known information providers: Insight Guides, whose titles have set the standard for visual travel guides since 1970, and Discovery Channel, the world's premier source of nonfiction television programming.

# Star Attractions

An instant reference to some of Rio de Janeiro's most popular tourist attractions to help you set your priorities.

*Sugar Loaf p20*

*Trem do Corcovado p22*

*Copacabana Beach p25*

*Botanical Gardens p32*

*Igreja de Santo Antônio p44*

*Mosteiro de São Bento p52*

*Museu de Arte Contemporânea p64*

*Parque Nacional da Tijuca, p8 and p90*

*Búzios p67*

*Cristo Redentor p22*

*Parati p69*

# RIO DE JANEIRO

## Introduction

## Places

## Culture

## Leisure

## Practical Information

# Rio de Janeiro – The Marvelous City

Opposite: Corcovado dominates the city; Sugar Loaf in the background

Think of Brazil and you think of Rio de Janeiro, a city which offers a little of everything that is best about a country that is the fifth largest in the world in terms of both size and population. How many other cities can pride themselves on offering miles of superb beaches, a tropical forest, beautiful mountains and all the infrastructure travelers come to expect from a major cosmopolitan city?

For its resident population, called the Cariocas, Rio is the *Cidade Maravilhosa*, the Marvelous City. It is imbued with a festive mood, not just during Carnival or the World Cup, but throughout the year. For those who like nightlife, Rio has world-class nightclubs, theaters and bars and, from famous venues to street-corner cafés, some of the world's most sophisticated and passionate music can be heard wafting through the air. Eating out is another major pre-occupation of the Cariocas, so visitors can expect the best in this department too. The residents are passionate about their sport, so Rio is a sporting paradise, not only for competitors, but also for those who like to watch. Almost any sport can be found here, but there are no prizes for guessing the favorite. Soccer, of course, and as well as being played on the beach, it can be seen at its best in the world's biggest stadium, Maracanã.

*Fun times*

**5**

*A packed Maracanã Stadium*

Rio, the world city. It has a ring, yet when the European explorers first arrived at the start of the 16th century, they were not very interested when they found only savage Indians and virgin forest. Among the explorers were part of a fleet sailing under the patronage of the Portuguese King, Dom Manuel I. It arrived in the giant bay in January 1502, two years after the discovery of Brazil, and the sailors, assuming it was the mouth of a big river, called it Rio de Janeiro, River of January. The name stuck.

Despite Portuguese interests, the first real settlers of any number in the Rio area are generally accepted to have been the French in 1555, when 600 of them disembarked close to what is now downtown. It would take the Portuguese 12 years to expel them, although the French did return in 1710 to put the city, then with major gold interests, under siege and claim a ransom before finally leaving it to the Portuguese a year later.

France's other key role in the development of Rio was Napoleon Bonaparte's expansionary plans in Europe which resulted in the Portuguese royal family – and virtually the entire Portuguese Court of some 15,000 nobles – fleeing to Rio in 1808 to avoid Napoleon's advancing army. The presence of the royal family resulted in Brazil remaining a kingdom until 1889 while most of Spanish-dominated South America was already republics by the first quarter of the 19th century. The presence of the

*Copacabana girl*

monarchy also resulted in the rapid development of Rio. Just the eight-month period following the arrival of the Portuguese Court saw the creation of the Supreme Military Court, the Law Courts, the Naval Academy, the Gunpowder Factory, the Schools of Medicine and Surgery, the Royal Printing Works, the first Brazilian newspaper, the Botanical Gardens and the Bank of Brazil.

Over the years Rio has grown to become one of the most important cities and ports, economically and politically, in South America, and remains so today. In the early 1900s, with the opening of the tunnels that gave access to the beaches along the Atlantic coast, and the building of the Copacabana Palace Hotel, the first deluxe five-star hotel in South America, Rio became a popular resort and destination for the world's rich and famous. The release in 1933 of the film *Flying Down to Rio*, with Fred Astaire, helped assure its universal fame. Since then, Rio has featured in many other famous films and songs, like the early-1960s *Garota de Ipanema* (*The Girl from Ipanema*), a tune that has become one of the most recorded of all time and come to epitomize the laid-back nature of the city, its residents and their *bossa nova* rhythm.

*A fashion-conscious city*

## Location and size

Located on the Atlantic coast, Rio de Janeiro is just 100km (62 miles) north of the Tropic of Capricorn, and about 2,400km (1,500 miles) south of the Equator. Rio is the world's largest tropical city, covering an area of 1,171 sq km (452 sq miles), and is home to a population of around 11 million. The second-largest Brazilian city and the country's third-busiest port, Rio is the capital of the state of Rio de Janeiro, one of the smallest states in the Republic with only 43,305 sq km (16,720 sq miles), yet still roughly the size of Denmark, Holland or Switzerland.

Rio, the city, is divided into three regions, geographically and demographically: Zona Norte (North Zone), Zona Sul (South Zone) and the rapidly developing and expanding Zona Oeste (West Zone), with the Maciço da Tijuca-Carioca Mountains in the middle. These are very steep mountains that include the Parque Nacional da Tijuca, and descend to the edge of the city center where the north and south zones meet. The majority of the inhabitants live in the Zona Norte; but visitors will spend most of their time in the Zona Sul which includes the main beaches and hotels, most of the city's middle- and upper-class homes and, ironically, many of the city's larger shanty towns, the *favelas*. The developing Zona Oeste contains two national parks, some of Rio's loveliest beaches and many new housing and shopping developments. This is where the city will

*City contrasts*

6

*Fishermen on the beach*

expand to in the future as the open, flat land beyond the mountains makes large developments, and the infrastructure to support them, possible.

The quickest way to become familiar with the city's geography is to ascend Corcovado Mountain, to the statue of Christ (*see page 22*), from where you can see arguably the most beautiful cityscape in the world. With views of both Zona Norte and Zona Sul, it gives some idea of how the population to date has managed to squeeze into the spaces between mountain and sea.

## Climate and when to go

Located in the tropics, the climate of the city of Rio is hot and humid, but never unbearably so, even at the height of summer. However, in the environs of Rio state there are many temperature variations, as the mountains, forest and sea all have their influence on the climate. These differences give the visitors multiple options, including the much cooler temperatures provided by the highland Imperial City of Petrópolis (*see page 65*).

*Forest in the city*

The average temperature in the city of Rio in summer (which being in the southern hemisphere runs from December through to March) is 25°C (77°F), but can climb on very hot days to a hot and humid 42°C (107°F). During this period there are numerous tropical storms which can be very heavy but rarely last for long. After a few minutes they clear, leaving either a beautiful, sunny day or a clear, starry night.

In winter (June to August) the temperature can drop to 16°C (61°F), but the average is nearer to 20°C (68°F). This is also the dry season, and a good time to visit Rio. From New Year to Carnival (the week before Lent) and on into March, the main local holiday season, the beaches are packed and hotel prices generally higher than the less frenetic winter season.

*Cooling off on Copacabana*

*Back to nature in the Parque Nacional da Tijuca*

*Botanical delights*

## Environment

Big cities, by definition, are not environmentally friendly. But Rio would appear to have found an ecological equilibrium with its lakes, beaches, the ocean and the largest urban forest and park in the world all mixed within the confines of an urban environment. Indeed, since it hosted the United Nations Conference on Environment and Development in June 1992 (the Earth Summit), Rio has been considered the planet's 'ecological capital'.

The Federal Government has invested billions to improve Rio's infrastructure, while the mayor's office is looking at projects to provide the city's *favelas* (shanty towns, *see page 12*) with basic sanitation, better schooling, community centers and health care for people of low incomes. The city is also facing up to the environmental challenges by developing 'Rio Cidade', an urban-recovery plan designed to preserve and sustain the biggest tropical metropolis of the southern hemisphere for future generations.

Among the highlights for visitors to Rio is the Parque Nacional da Tijuca, the largest urban forest in the world. Much of the forest was a coffee plantation until the mid-19th century when it was reforested to guarantee the city's water supply. By 1887 more than 100,000 new trees had been planted. Today it has hundreds of species of plants, along with jacaranda, *jaqueira*, ironwood and *pau Brasil*. Some of the trees grow to over 30m (100ft) high. The forest is home to many endangered animals such as the golden-lion tamarin monkey, *sagui* and *macaco-prego* monkeys, spiders, snakes, wild dogs and cats and many species of birds. (For tour details, *see page 90*.)

Down at sea level, close to the main hotels, is the city's exceptional Botanical Gardens (*see page 32*), where thousands of species of herbs, fruits and trees grow, and which has been designated by UNESCO as a Biosphere Reserve.

## The Cariocas

During one of the first expeditions to Rio the European explorers built a white house by the river. The local Indian tribe called it 'Carioca', meaning house of white people, and henceforth this became the name used for the inhabitants of Rio de Janeiro.

The Carioca is one of the most mixed races in Brazil, with the influence of Indians, Africans and Europeans. The Portuguese themselves are a mixture of Lusitano, Roman and Arabic races; during the colonization times, as only a few Portuguese women came to a new colony, the men developed relations with local Indian and African women. However, the 'whites' have always occupied a better position in Brazilian society than the people who were descended from African slaves and Indians, and even today this divide is defined.

*Surfers at Arpoador Beach*

Fortunately, Brazil has never had racial segregation laws or white supremacist movements, such as existed in the USA or South Africa. Today, despite the enormous socio-economic gap between racial groups in different areas, there appears to be little, if any, racial tension – helped, no doubt, by the success of so many black soccer players, such as Pelé, and entertainers.

9

All Cariocas are recognized for their warmth, friendliness, love of their beaches and particularly their laid-back attitude to life. Time becomes a flexible concept when in Rio, and it is nothing for a true Carioca to arrive an hour or two late for dinner or a business meeting. Brazilians also consider body contact a fundamental part of a conversation. When greeting, be prepared to be kissed on both cheeks by a member of the opposite sex. Women kiss other women, and men often embrace each other (although they never actually kiss).

*Hanging loose at Feira Hippie*

In general, Brazilians are very receptive to meeting foreigners, but their laid-back attitude can sometimes extend to asking quite personal questions. These should not be taken as prying, however, but as a genuine desire to understand you.

## Language

The official language in Brazil is Portuguese, although the accent, delivery and phraseology are noticeably different from those used in Portugal. There are also more than 100 known Indian languages spoken in Brazil, and others are still to be discovered. By popular demand, the second language now taught in schools is English. Spanish has been gaining popularity since the Mercosul – the South American trading partnership similar to the EU – was created, and the government has been giving incentives to schools to teach it. Educated Brazilians are generally able to understand quite a bit of Spanish without actually

*A statue of St Antony*

*New Year's Eve Festival*

*Gay abandon*

speaking it and a hybrid language, called Portunhol, has developed over the years.

Many people in Rio speak some English (particularly in first-class hotels, restaurants and the better shops), but Brazilians are very tolerant and helpful with people who try but don't speak their language correctly.

## Religion

In 1980 a survey found that nearly 90 percent of Brazilians declared their religion as Roman Catholic, making it the world's largest Catholic country. That percentage will have changed noticeably over the past two decades with the growth of evangelical groups fronted by charismatic TV preachers, as well as all the traditional and new Protestant religions. There are no restrictions on religious worship anywhere in Brazil.

Though Roman Catholicism is the 'official' religion, a number of religious groups do use aspects of the Catholic faith mixed in with rituals that would seem bizarre to the Vatican. Candomblé was brought by African slaves who were castigated for their heathen ways by their masters and the Jesuit priests. To be able to perform their traditional ceremonies, the slaves mixed parts of the Catholic ceremonies in with theirs. The Catholic Church hoped the African religions would die out. However, Candomblé, and Umbanda, a religion derived from it, are still practiced all over Brazil and are at their most visible in Rio during the New Year celebrations.

## Carnival

Carnival in Rio is one of the world's great events. For the week before Lent leading up to Ash Wednesday, rich and poor, black and white, men and women, gay and straight enjoy themselves in a celebration that dates back to the ancient Romans and Greeks. Carnival arrived in Brazil from Portugal with costume balls and parades for royalty and the nobility. The African slaves performed their own humbler style of Carnival, when one of the men would dress as king for the day. This tradition has carried on until today with the character known as Rei Momo, King of Polygamy, reigning over the celebrations.

A grand ball in the Venetian style was held in 1840 with masks, streamers and confetti. This brought an element of style to Carnival that became popular and is reflected today in the big balls held in clubs and hotels. Carnival societies were formed to organize parades with singing, dancing and fancy dress. The now famous samba beat resulted from a suggestion by a Carnival club organizer that all the drummers should play at the same time. The first *escola de samba* (samba school, *see page 72*) appeared in 1920, named Deixa Falar (Let 'em Talk), when the blacks who came from Bahia in the 19th century introduced a traditional folk music based on the rhythm of the drum.

The early Carnival parades on Praça XV in downtown Rio were lively affairs in which the Bahian women, with huge, billowing dresses, formed a cordon within which the samba dancers performed. Today Carnival is an enormous affair, bigger in fact than the ship-building industry. Samba schools in most of the poor areas of Rio employ an estimated 80,000 people full time, with over 500,000 additional jobs generated during the preceding three months. These schools compete to be the best in parades organized around the city, and in the specially designed Passarela do Samba (also known as the Sambódromo) Stadium in downtown Rio the *crème de la crème* come together to choose the ultimate champion.

*Leading the parade*

Some samba schools spend as much as US$4million on the parade, much of which is money gained from the *bicheiros*, the bosses and bankers of Rio's illegal 'animal numbers gambling game'. This lottery, in which bets are placed on numbered 'animals', was originally a legitimate form of gambling to raise money for the city's zoo. But once the revenue was found for the zoo, it became a black-market game, tolerated because it ploughs cash into the Carnival. Although the *bicheiros* are major backers of the Carnival, using the event to launder money and improve their public image, many large national and international companies now donate too. They have been encouraged to do so to allow schools to get away from some of their more questionable forms of financing.

*Pearly queen Rio style*

**11**

Rio's Carnival attracts Brazilian stars and personalities to take part in their favorite school's parade, and many international celebrities can be spotted in the boxes watching the parades unfold. Each school is a parade in its own right, with the biggest featuring over 4,000 participants

*Samba school participants*

whom they have to get from one end of the Sambódromo to the other in around 80 minutes. All the schools have their own theme – a different one each year – around which the samba is written and the action played out. A Carnival parade is pure theater, but theater on the move.

## Population growth and the favelas

Space has always been at a premium in Rio. Improvizing a place to live started with the arrival of the Portuguese royal family and its entourage of 15,000 in 1808. Rio, which then had 50,000 inhabitants, saw a 30 percent growth in its population overnight and nowhere to put them. By 1840 the population had swelled to more than 800,000, a 16-fold increase in just 30 years. At the time there were few options for the poor and unskilled in Rio. They could live in a small room in the city center, called a *cortiço*, or in better housing away from the center but endure poor and expensive transport facilities. The only other alternative was to construct an 'illegal' house on a hillside where no one else wanted to live. It was the beginning of the *favelas*, an aspect of Rio that is almost as well known as the Sugar Loaf mountain.

The first 'formal' *favela* appeared on the Morro da Providencia (Providence Hill) at the end of the 19th century. It was started by a group of soldiers who had fought in the Canudos War in the state of Bahia. Returning to Rio, and receiving no assistance from the government for rehousing, they built on the hill. The word *favela* comes from a plant that grows on the hillsides in Bahia.

*Bar in Favela Vila Canoas*

*Favela Rocinha*

Today most of the established shanty towns have a well-organized social structure and running water and electricity. Rocinha, which sprang up in the 1940s overlooking Gávea and São Conrado, is a good example. It has an estimated population of 80,000, making it the largest *favela* in Brazil. Most are ordinary people who want a place of their own that is close to their job and, despite the difficulties, residents have been able to create their own way of life and protect their dignity. The biggest problem they face is drug dealers who have made parts of the *favelas* no-go areas, even for the police. Outsiders may unwittingly walk into one of these areas, so if you wish to learn more about the *favelas* you should go on an organized tour, such as the one at Rocinha (*see pages 31 and 90*).

## Economy and industry

Rio is located in Brazil's southeast, the country's most developed region where 32 percent of the population live; 65 percent of the industrial products are manufactured, together with 65 percent of Brazil's service industries and 40 percent of agricultural production. Seventy percent of Brazil's imports and exports are shipped to and from the southeast of Brazil, and almost 85 percent of travelers, national and international, embark or disembark here.

Many boom or bust cycles have marked the economic history of Brazil. In colonial times Rio and Salvador were the two most important cities, with the economy based on the exploitation of a single export: tropical hard wood. In the 16th century sugar cane became important, and by the beginning of the 18th century precious minerals, gold, silver and diamonds were mined in the neighboring state of Minas Gerais and exported to Europe through the port of Rio. This created a large sector of commerce dealing with jewelry, which changed Rio's economy for ever. Today the city is still considered one of the world's most important trading centers for precious stones. Finally, in the 19th and at beginning of the 20th century, coffee brought prosperity to the city and much of the southeast.

*Diamonds are a girl's best friend*

The State of Rio at the start of the new millennium is important in terms of Brazil's industrial base. Modern industrial growth started during World War I and in the 1940s the first steel plant was constructed. The city is an influential financial center – alongside São Paulo – and one of the most popular venues for conferences and conventions in Latin America. Commerce is concentrated mainly around the large shopping centers, tourism and the 'clean industries' of banking, law, accounting, publishing, telecommunications and insurance. Most of Brazil's record and film companies are based in Rio, close to Latin America's largest media concern, Globo. The city is also the most important center for fashion design in South America. Rio is a notable cultural capital, too. Its many museums, historic buildings, libraries, cinemas, galleries, theaters and show houses attract millions of people to the city every year, all of whom in their turn contribute to the local economy.

**13**

*Tourists at Quinta da Boa Vista*

# Historical Highlights

**1500** Brazil is discovered by Pedro Álvares Cabral, a Portuguese explorer on his way to India, after his ship is blown off course.

**1502** On 1 January an expedition enters Guanabara Bay. Sailors mistake it for a river mouth, naming it Rio de Janeiro, River of January.

**1504** Second Portuguese expedition arrives in Guanabara Bay to occupy the new territory and make contact with the native people.

**1519** Ferdinand Magellan's expedition to circumnavigate the globe. He stays for 14 days.

**1555** French expedition commanded by Nicolau Durand Villegaignon arrives in Guanabara Bay and founds a colony of French Calvinists. A fort is built and two years later the position is reinforced with a further 1,000 French settlers.

**1560** Mem de Sá, the third Governor General, destroys the French fort. But the French remain, and with the local Tamoios Indian tribe occupy other areas of the bay now known as Flamengo.

**1565** Estácio de Sá (nephew of Mem de Sá) arrives with reinforcements from Portugal to fight the French and their native allies.

**1567** Mem de Sá advises his nephew to organize an expedition and on 20 January (São Sebastião's Day) he manages, with help of the Araribóia Indians, to drive out the French. Estácio de Sá is wounded and dies a month later.

**1608** The religious orders start building in the city. The Franciscans on the Santo Antônio Hill, Carmelites in Praça XV, Benedictines on the São Bento Hill, and Jesuits on the Castelo Hill. They have great political and economic power.

**1693** Discovery of major gold deposits in Minas Gerais state (General Mines) starts a huge migration of people from every part of Brazil. Strategically placed, Rio becomes the main port through which the gold and supplies are shipped.

**1710** The French lay siege to Rio, and succeed in the second attempt – in 1711 – under Rene Duguay-Trouin who commands more than 5,000 soldiers. The French take the city and only leave after a heavy ransom has been paid.

**1724** The construction of Arco da Lapa, which commenced in 1673, is completed, bringing water from the Carioca River in Santa Teresa to a fountain in Largo da Carioca.

**1763** Rio becomes the capital city of the Vice-Royalty of Brazil, which helps bring prosperity to the new city and its 50,000 population.

**1808** The Portuguese Prince Regent, Dom João, his mother, Queen Maria I, along with 15,000 of their Court, leave Portugal for Rio due to the threat of invasion by Napoleon Bonaparte.

**1815** Brazil becomes part of the United Kingdom of Portugal and Algarve, with Rio the capital.

**1816** With the death of Queen Maria, her son becomes Dom João VI, King of Portugal, Brazil and Algarve. As there is no more threat from Napoleon, the Court now asks that he return to Portugal.

**1821** Dom João VI is forced back to Portugal and leaves the colony in the hands of his 22-year-old son, Pedro, who becomes Prince Regent.

**1822** O Dia do Fico (the Day of the Stay). On 7 September, during a visit to São Paulo, Dom Pedro declares the independence of Brazil. He is named Emperor and Perpetual Defender.

**1831** Dom Pedro abdicates the Brazilian throne in favour of his five-year-old-son, Dom Pedro de Alcântara, and returns to Europe.

**1840** After years of instability that threatened to split the country, the Brazilian born Dom Pedro II takes the throne on reaching 15 years of age. Industrial development is rapid, bringing gas lamps and improved sanitary systems.

**1845** Dom Pedro II builds a Summer Palace in Petrópolis.

**1858** Opening of the railway station, Estrada de Ferro Dom Pedro II (now Central do Brasil).

**1876** A telephone link is installed between Rio and Petrópolis, two years after Dom Pedro II met Alexander Graham Bell at an exhibition.

**1885** A small railway to the summit of Corcovado is inaugurated.

**1888** While Dom Pedro II is in Europe, his daughter and acting regent Princess Isabel introduces the Lei Áurea (abolition of slavery law).

**1889** After a bloodless coup, headed by Marechal Manuel Deodoro da Fonseca, Dom Pedro II and the royal family are exiled to Europe. Rio de Janeiro becomes the capital of the Republic and Fonseca the Republic's first President.

**1892** A tunnel opens, giving easy access to Copacabana from the rest of Rio.

**1902** The mayor, Pereira Passos, an engineer who studied in Paris, starts the grand transformation of Rio de Janeiro, 'Rio da Belle Époque'.

**1923** The Copacabana Palace Hotel opens.

**1925** The newspaper *O Globo* is published for the first time. It lays the foundation for a media empire that is one of the world's largest today .

**1926** The new Jockey Club opens.

**1931** The statue of Christ the Redeemer is inaugurated on Corcovado.

**1946** Gambling is outlawed.

**1950** Maracanã Stadium is completedfor the fourth soccer World Cup, the first after Word War II. Brazil lose 2-1 to Uruguay in the final.

**1958** Brazil's soccer team wins its first World Cup, beating Sweden 5-2 in the final. It retains the cup in 1962 and becomes the first three-time winner in 1970.

**1960** President Jucelino Kubitschek transfers the capital from Rio de Janeiro to Brasília. Rio becomes capital of a new Guanabara State

**1964** The military seizes power after political instability. The foundation stone is laid for a new Metropolitan Cathedral.

**1966** The first Hippie Market is established in Ipanema.

**1967** A new tunnel is inaugurated connecting the Lagoa, Cosme Velho and Rio Comprido.

**1969** Pelé scores his 1,000th professional goal at the Maracanã Stadium.

**1972** A cable car system is inaugurated for Sugar Loaf. Emerson Fittipaldi becomes the first Brazilian Formula One World Drivers' Champion. He repeats the performance in 1974 and is followed by Nelson Piquet (1981, 1983, 1987) and Ayrton Senna (1988, 1990, 1991).

**1974** The Rio-Niterói bridge opens.

**1975** Rio becomes the capital of a new unified Rio de Janeiro State.

**1980** Rio's first major shopping center, Rio Sul, opens to be followed a year later by Barra Shopping which by 1994 has become the largest shopping complex in Latin America.

**1985** The military abdicate power. A democratically elected president, Tancredo Neves, wins the election, but Vice President José Sarney takes office when Neves dies soon afterwards. Rock 'n' Rio, a massive week-long rock festival, takes place in Barra da Tijuca. It will be six years before Rock 'n' Rio II is held in Maracanã Stadium.

**1990** Paul McCartney plays to a crowd of over 180,000 in Maracanã Stadium. It is the largest paying public ever for a single act.

**1992** The Earth Summit. Rio de Janeiro is the venue for the United Nations Conference on Environment and Development, bringing together the largest-ever gathering of heads of state and government (a total of 122) to discuss the future of the planet.

**1994** Brazil becomes the first four-times winner of the soccer World Cup, defeating Italy on penalties in the final.

**1999** 'The Great Train Robber' Ronald Biggs, sentenced to 30 years' prison in 1963, celebrates his 70th birthday, still safe from the clutches of the British law after escaping to Rio on 1970.

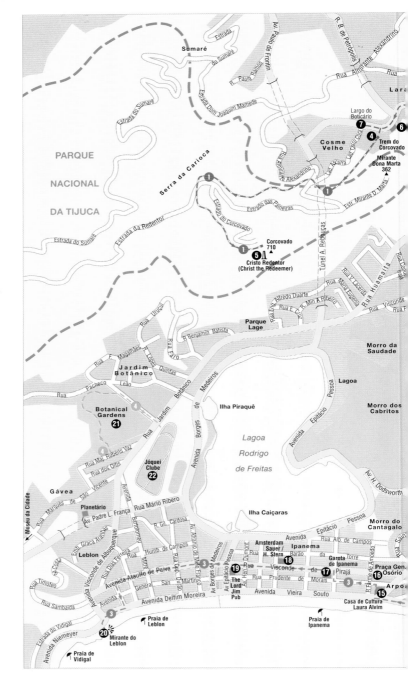

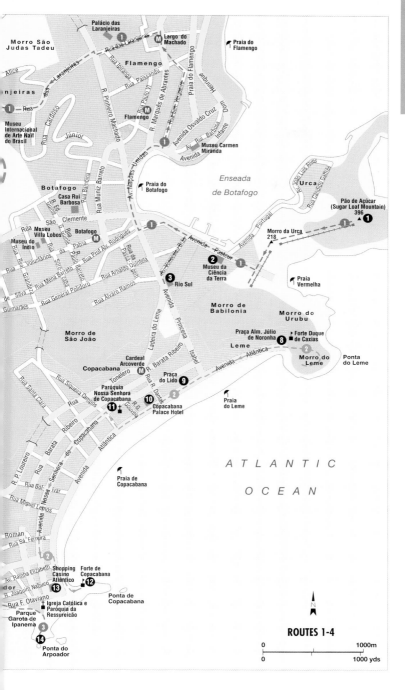

*Botafogo Bay with Sugar Loaf in the background*

*Preceding pages: Copacabana*

*Christ the Redeemer*

*A beautiful backdrop*

# Route 1

## The Landmarks: Sugar Loaf and Corcovado

**Pão de Açúcar – Museu da Ciência da Terra – Shopping Rio Sul – Bica da Rainha – Trem do Corcovado – Cristo Redentor – Museu Internacional de Arte Naïf – Largo do Boticário** *See map on pages 18–19*

Rio de Janeiro boasts two globally recognized landmarks: the mountains of Sugar Loaf (Pão de Açúcar) and Corcovado, the latter's peak being home to the statue of Christ the Redeemer (Christo Redentor), his arms outstretched to 'embrace the city'. Route 1 includes a cable car ride to the top of Sugar Loaf, with its spectacular views over the bay and Copacabana Beach, and then a drive through the streets of Botafogo, Laranjeiras and Cosme Velho and the ride of a lifetime on one of the world's great mountain railways to the top of Corcovado. The two mountains are highly recommended for all visitors, but, in between, the route also takes in part of Rio's historic past, from prehistoric origins at the Science Museum (Museu da Ciência da Terra) to the delightful colonial square of Largo do Boticário. Art lovers are in for a treat with a tour of a unique museum concentrating on the Brazilian passion for naïve art.

When the Portuguese arrived in Rio they asked the local Indian Tupi-Guarani tribe what the mountain at the mouth of Guanabara Bay was called. The reply was '*Pau-nh-Acuqua*', which translates as 'high-hill, pointed and isolated', but the name sounded very much lot like the Portuguese '*Pão de Açúcar*' (sugar loaf). As the peak looked like the clay molds they used to cast refined sugar into a conical lump called a sugar loaf, the name stuck, and the distinctive mountain became one of the world's most famous landmarks.

The first cable car to ★★★ **Pão de Açúcar (Sugar Loaf)** ❶ (buses. 107, 500, 511, 512, daily 8am–10pm, runs every 30 minutes) was constructed in 1912, but was replaced by the one that runs today in 1972. The first stage from Praça General Tibúrcio travels 575m (1,900ft), and climbs 220m (720ft) in three minutes up to Morro da Urca. The cable car has enough space for 75 passengers in its bubble-like *'bondinho'*. At Morro da Urca there is a café, theater, souvenir shop, photography shop and an excellent, if expensive, restaurant. There is also a heliport for sightseeing flights around Rio (Helisight, tel: 511 2141; flights from about R\$50,00).

*Arriving at the top*

The second stage of the cable car goes 760m (2,500ft) in three minutes to the summit of Sugar Loaf, which is 396m (1,299ft) high. The view is spectacular. In one direction is Guanabara Bay, the Centro area of downtown Rio and the Rio-Niterói bridge; in another, Corcovado Mountain and its statue of Christ; and in another, the Atlantic Ocean and sensuous curve of Copacabana Beach.

There are a number of trails leading down from the summit, which allow visitors to slip away from the main tourist areas and enjoy the flora and fauna of this strange rock. Stay as long as you like – the return ticket has no time limit. There are even picnic tables for people who bring their own lunch. It is also possible to climb the rock with the right equipment, or walk up to the first stage with a guide (try Carlos Millan, tel: 522 5586 or 9966 7010).

*Praia Vermelha*

On the way down from Morro da Urca you'll see **Praia Vermelha**, to the left of the base station, so named because the sand is redder than on the other beaches. At the bottom there is a souvenir shop and the Roda Viva *churrascaria* (barbecue) restaurant that holds traditional live shows for tourists (tel: 295 4045). Ronald Biggs, who fled to Rio after stealing £2.6 million from a London to Glasgow mail train, was kidnapped here in 1981 by mercenaries who tried, but failed, to return him to Britain for trial.

Walk along Avenida Pasteur and on the left is **Museu da Ciência da Terra** ❷ (Avenida Pasteur 404, tel: 295 0032 ex 438, Monday to Friday 10am–4pm). The impressive building, with lion sculptures out front, was intended to be Brazil's first university but became the state's export department when it was completed in 1908. Now a science museum, it houses over 5,000 geological samples, including crystals, and meteorites. There is also a paleontology room, with the skeleton of a 225 million-year-old reptile.

*Museu da Ciência da Terra*

Continue along Avenida Pasteur past the **Instituto Benjamin Constant**, built in 1872 on land donated by

Dom Pedro II, who founded the Imperial Institute for blind children. On the opposite side of the road is the exclusive **Iate Clube do Rio de Janeiro (Rio Yacht Club)**.

On the next corner is the Federal University. Turn left into Avenida Venceslau Brás and head past the hospital. Continue round to the left, past Canecão, one of the most famous venues for shows in Brazil (tel: 543 1241 for listings), to **Shopping Rio Sul** ❸ (tel: 545 7200; 10am–10pm). This is an excellent center, worth a look even if you don't want to buy. The Praça da Alimentação (Food Hall) is on the second floor, and the center has five cinemas as well as a gym and nightclub.

From here take bus No. 569 or 583 to Cosme Velho. This takes you through the streets of Botafogo, Laranjeiras and Cosme Velho, and stops just before the terminus (ask the driver). Across the road (381 Rua Cosme Velho) is the **Bica da Rainha** (Queen's Tap). Queen Maria I of Portugal used to come here to take the therapeutic waters in the early 19th century.

*Bica da Rainha*

*Trem do Corcovado*

**22**

Walk up the hill a short distance for the ★ **Trem do Corcovado** (Corcovado Mountain Train) ❹ (Praça São Judas Tadeu, daily 9am–6pm every 30 minutes, price includes entry to the Parque Nacional da Tijuca to visit the statue of Christ, and to the Naïve Art Museum, described opposite). The rail service travels through the forest for 3.8km (2½ miles) up Corcovado (Hunchback) Mountain. It works by means of a rack and pinion mechanism on the track, and the 36-tonne train takes 20 minutes to climb to the top at 15kph (9mph). When the service started in 1884, with Dom Pedro II its first illustrious passenger, the trains were steam and considered an engineering miracle. In 1910 the line became Brazil's first electric railway, and was used to transport the pieces of the statue of Christ over a period of four years.

At the top is ★★★ **Cristo Redentor** (Christ the Redeemer) ❺ (Parque Nacional da Tijuca, daily 8.30am–6.30pm). Facing east, the statue of stands 710m (2,330ft) above the city. Inaugurated in 1931, it weighs 1,145 tonnes and stands 30m (100ft) high on the top of its own chapel which adds another 8m (26ft) to its height. The chapel is dedicated to Nossa Senhora da Aparecida do Norte, the patron saint of Brazil, and a copy of her famous small black wooden statue can be seen inside. (Mass, Sunday 11.30am.) The interior of the giant statue is concrete, but the outer layer is soapstone. The statue was designed and engineered by Heitor da Silva Costa, with the collaboration of the French sculptor Pierre Landowski, who was responsible for the hands and face.

The view from the top is spectacular and confirms Rio's claim to be the most beautiful city in the world. Directly

*Christ embraces the city*

in front is Sugar Loaf, with Botafogo in the foreground. To the left is the downtown area, and to Christ's right can just be seen the beaches of Copacabana and Ipanema, with Lagoa Rodrigo de Freitas, Leblon, the Jockey Club and Botanical Gardens down to the far right.

Return by train to the Cosme Velho station and walk up the hill to the ★★ **Museu Internacional de Arte Naïf do Brasil** ❻ (Rua Cosme Velho 561; tel: 205 8612; Tuesday to Friday 10am–6pm, Saturday and Sunday noon–6pm; price can be included in your Corcovado ticket). With over 8,000 paintings from Brazil and 130 other countries, the museum houses the most comprehensive collection of naïve art in the world. Naïve painters are usually self taught, and not linked with any school, so the selection here is wide and varied. Naïve paintings appear in most important books about Brazil, and no major exhibition is held on the subject without Brazilian naïves.

*Museu Internacional de Arte Naïf do Brazil*

The collection in Cosme Velho dates from 1320 with the Iranian painting *A Batalha de Torbalá* (the Martyrdom of Hussein) and ranges up to the present day. The paintings provide a history of naïve art and include the largest naïve canvas in the world. Painted by Lia Mittarakis, and measuring 4m x 7m (13ft x 23ft), it depicts the city of Rio.

**23**

Walk up Rua Cosme Velho, and near the top end of the road, on your right, is **Largo do Boticário** ❼ (free access any time), a small cobbled neo-colonial square with graceful residences that have been faithfully restored to their former beauty. It is named Boticário (Chemist) after the pharmacist Joaquim José da Silva Souto, who moved here in 1831. He became famous for his syrups and was the Royal Apothecary. The square has seven houses and a fountain, installed in 1848, supplied with water from the Carioca River, which can still be seen running under the bridge at the entrance. The local Tamoyos Indian tribe believed that the river held magical powers to make women beautiful and men virile. The house on the corner, No.1, was the workshop and residence of the painter Augusto Rodrigues (1913–93), founder of the Escolinha de Arte do Brasil (Brazilian School of Art).

*Largo do Boticário, facade detail*

Return to the hotel either by bus or taxi. It is also possible to do a deal with a taxi driver to stay with you for the entire route, an option that is cheaper than you might imagine; he will take you to Sugar Loaf, wait at the bottom while you explore, and then continue through the forest up to the peak of Corcovado Mountain, wait in the car park, and return you to the hotel. There is also a good selection of tour companies who run tours to all the main sites of Rio and beyond, and most of the car rental agencies can organize drivers (*see Getting Around on page 86*).

# Route 2

*Bungey bouncing at the beach*

Copacabana – The World's Most Famous Beach

**Avenida Atlântica – Avenida Nossa Senhora de Copacabana – Forte de Copacabana – Colônia dos Pescadores – Casino Atlântico** *See map on pages 18–19*

Brazilians are proud of the world's most famous beach, yet the name is not even a Brazilian word, but Bolivian. It comes from the small village of Copacabana near Lake Titicaca, and is derived from an ancient Amerindian language, Quechua, still spoken in Peru (*Copa Caguana* means 'Luminous Place'). In the 17th century Peruvian traders passed through this village and brought the name to Rio. Later, along with Portuguese and Bolivian traders, they erected an image of Nossa Senhora de Copacabana (Our Lady of Copacabana) on a small stone hill which separated the beaches of Ipanema and what is now Copacabana. In 1746 a church was built on the site but it was demolished at the beginning of the 20th century.

The beach occupies a vast crescent between the rocky promontory of Morro do Leme at one end and the peninsular that is a fort at the other. In the early days it was virtually inaccessible because of the mountains and the only inhabitants were fishermen. But all that changed in 1892, when a tunnel was cut through the rock. The Túnel Velho (Old Tunnel) was serviced by horse-drawn trams, then in 1904 the Túnel Novo (New Tunnel) was made and electric trams linked Copacabana to Botafogo. The Avenida Atlântica beachfront was constructed and the area witnessed explosive growth. Neoclassical and Art Nouveau palaces sprang up, first to four floors and later 12. Sadly these have now been rebuilt as apartment blocks.

In 1923 South America's first five-star hotel was opened on Avenida Atlântica. The Copacabana Palace Hotel was the meeting place for artists, politicians, intellectuals and the rich and famous in the 1950s and 1960s, and became a symbol for everything sophisticated.

Today Copacabana may not be as clean and sophisticated as neighboring Ipanema, but it has everything that makes up a small city. It is possible to spend a week in Rio without ever leaving Copacabana except to return to the airport. The beach is the focal point of the city's New Year celebrations and many millions of Cariocas come here, predominantly dressed in white, to see the year in and enjoy one of the world's most spectacular fireworks displays. All the hotels host elaborate balls and dinners.

*Fireworks on New Year's Eve*

At the Sugar Loaf end of the beach, at the northeast corner of Leme Beach, is **Praça Alm. Júlio de Noronha ❽**. A

craft fair is held here on Sundays, with skating and model car hire for children. There is also the **Caminho dos Pescadores**, a walkway built in 1985 around the base of the Morro do Leme. Be careful of fishermen casting their lines, as the walkway is quite narrow in places.

*Copacabana creatures*

Walk along Avenida Atlântica – on the beach side there are kiosks serving beer, coconut juice, soft drinks and so on – to Avenida Princesa Isabel. This is the point where Leme Beach becomes ★★★ **Copacabana Beach**. On the corner is one of Rio's best well-known hotels, the **Méridien Copacabana** (*see page 94*), which opened in 1975. Towering 37 stories above the beach, the rooftop restaurant of the Méridien, ★ **Le Saint Honoré** (*see page 78*), is outstanding, with spectacular views along the beach.

*Avenida Atlântica*

**25**

From this hotel down to the Copacabana Palace Hotel is an area that should be avoided by tourists at night. It is the heart of what is left of Rio's red-light district. During the day it is completely safe, however, and in the center, and bordering Avenida Atlântica, is **Praça do Lido** ❾, a quiet little square with a children's playground and school. You won't find the name Praça do Lido displayed anywhere, though, as the square was renamed about 30 years ago as Parque Irmãos Bernardelli, and has a sculpture of the Bernardelli brothers by artist H. Leão Velloso. People sit around playing cards, and the square has a good family atmosphere during the day.

*Volleyball in progress*

Continuing down the beach brings you to a large white building that looks like a giant wedding cake. This is the famous ★ **Copacabana Palace Hotel** ❿ (*see page 94*). The building did much to make the word Copacabana a household name after its facade was used as the backdrop to the 1933 film *Flying Down to Rio* (which paired Fred Astaire and Ginger Rogers for the first time).

The Copa, as it became known, was built in 1923, and has had many famous guests, Bill Clinton, Fidel Castro,

Errol Flynn and Orson Welles to name just a few. Brigitte Bardot also came here, as did Janis Joplin, plus Edward, Prince of Wales in 1931, and Diana, Princess of Wales in 1991. The hotel, which had gone through a decline in the 1970s, regained popularity when it was bought by Orient Express Hotels in 1989 and restored to its former glory. Like the Méridien, the Copacabana Palace houses one of the city's outstanding restaurants, the Cipriani (*see page 78*), named after the group's famous hotel in Venice.

Following the beach, but staying on the side with the buildings, turn right up Rua Hilário Gouveia. In one block this turns into **Praça Serzedelo Correia** where there is a children's playground and facilities for people to play chess. On the Hilário Gouveia side of the Praça is the parish church of Copacabana, **Paróquia Nossa Senhora de Copacabana ⑪**. Completed in 1977, this church has a very interesting roof illumination lighting a giant statue of Jesus. On the left is a chapel named Adoração do Santíssimo Sacramento, with paintings of the passage of Jesus' life. The whole front side the chapel comprises a stained-glass window wall by the Brazilian artist Barbieri Ribeiro.

*Emergency service*

*Colônia dos Pescadores*

*Forte de Copacabanca: exhibit in the Army Historical Museum*

You are now going to walk up Avenida Nossa Senhora de Copacabana against the flow of the traffic. This avenue has some exclusive, if dated, shops and gets very busy with traffic at times.

If you like old **fire stations** there is one worth seeing at the corner of Rua Xavier da Silveira and Rua Pompeu Loureiro. Usually the fire engines are lined up outside.

At Rua Sá Ferreira, turn left and walk one block to the beach. This area is known as *Posto Seis* (Post Six) because there are six lifeguard stations along the seafront starting with *Posto Um* at the end closest to Sugar Loaf.

Cross over to the beach side and continue towards the Forte de Copacabana and Sofitel Rio Palace Hotel. Just before the entrance to the fort, on the beach, is the **Colônia dos Pescadores** (Colony of Fishermen), where fish is landed every day. Notice a small shrine to St Peter.

At the southwestern end of the beach, the small peninsular known as Esquina da Igrejimha (Little Church's Corner) was a perfect location for the ★★ **Forte de Copacabana ⑫** (Tuesday to Sunday 10am–4pm; free on Wednesday), one of the forts guarding the entrance to Guanabara Bay. Built in 1914, it is now used as a training establishment, but houses a museum of general and military history.

Pass through the guardhouse and walk along the cobbled path lined with sweet-smelling almond trees and old cannons from around the world. Stop here and look along the beach for a spectacular view of Copacabana with the Sugar Loaf in the background. At the end of the path climb the stairs and cross the military bridge on to the cupola gun emplacement. The fort was furnished with six German-made cannons installed in four cupolas. The main large gun barrels were capable of firing shells up to 40km (25 miles). At the bottom of the stairs, it is possible to go inside the cupola to view the firing mechanism itself.

The fort, which is considered a feat of military engineering of that era, was also the stage for one of the most courageous events in the history of Brazil: the '18 of the Fort' (Dezoito do Forte). In 1922, in the time of the Old Republic when the coffee farmers of São Paulo and the cattle breeders of Minas Gerais took turns in power, the young officials of the armed forces began to question and oppose the power of the major rural producers. It was at Forte de Copacabana that the famous 18 of the Fort held out against over 700 heavily armed soldiers of the political opposition. Eventually realising that they could not win, they divided the national flag into 18 pieces and walked to the beach carrying the fragments on their chests. Only two of the group survived the 'walk of death': Siqueira Campos and Eduardo Gomes (who later became the minister of aviation).

*A feat of military engineering*

The **Historico de Exército** (Army Historical Museum) houses a huge collection showing the army's participation in every era since it was formed. Room sets with full-sized models wearing the original clothes of famous military personnel are laid out, while an interactive display gives explanations in several languages.

Opposite the entrance to the fort is **Sofitel Rio Palace Hotel** (*see page 94*) and the **Shopping Casino Atlântico** ⓭. The two sit on the site of a famous casino, which operated from 1942 until gambling was made illegal in Brazil in 1946. It fills the entire block between Avenida Atlântica and Avenida Nossa Senhora de Copacabana. Over 150 shops selling jewelry, precious stones and antiques can be found here. One worth visiting is Ivoticí on the second floor; owned by Dona Ivoticí Knoff, an artist who uses traditional Brazilian Indian art as her inspiration, it has a large collection of original native art.

*Buffet at the Sofitel Rio Palace and Casino Atlântico shopping*

At the back of the center turn left, and walk to Rua Francisco Otaviano 99 to see the **Igreja Católica e Paróquia da Ressurecião** (Monday 7am–1pm and 4–10pm; Tuesday 4–7pm; Wednesday, Thursday, Friday 7am–1pm and 4–10pm; Saturday 7am–11.30am and 4–7pm; Sunday 7am–1pm and 4–10pm). This modern church has a side chapel that is open to the elements.

Heading up Rua Francisco Otaviano, away from Copacabana Beach, will bring you to the beaches of Arpoador and Ipanema, close to where Route 3 begins.

*Ipanema from Ponta do Arpoador*

## Route 3

**Ipanema and Beyond**

**Ponta do Arpoador – Parque Garota de Ipanema – Praia Ipanema – Amsterdam Sauer and H.Stern – Lord Jim Pub – Leblon** *See map on pages 18–19*

*Ipanema, a place to see...*

*...and be seen*

In the 1960s the song *Garota de Ipanema* (*The Girl from Ipanema*) evoked the feeling of Rio's beach culture, and nowhere is that more prevalent today than in Ipanema itself. The name still conjures up the feeling of carefree days in the sun, and the area does not let the visitor down as it has one of the best stretches of beach in Rio (though Ipanema is actually an Indian word meaning 'bad water').

The district started to be urbanised after some construction work at the end of the 19th century but the building plots only became popular after 1902 with the arrival of trams. By the 1960s and 1970s, Ipanema was a swinging place. The beach, with light sand and clean water, was where artists and intellectuals met. The streets, especially around Praça Osório, were alive with the activities of artists and writers. Bars were watering holes for the *bossa nova* crowd, including composers Tom Jobim and Vinícius de Moraes who helped make Ipanema famous.

The gold, sun-tanned bodies of the Ipanema girls clad in their 'dental floss' bikinis ensured that the reputation of the beach spread, and soon it became the most famous and fashionable in Brazil. Ipanema's street corners, full of bronzed and beautiful people, began to dictate the fashion and behavior of a whole nation.

But today Ipanema is a sophisticated resort in its own right. The transversal streets that start by the sea and finish in Largo Rodrigo de Freitas are full of sweet-smelling trees which give the borough its distinct charm. The many kiosks along the beach are the meeting points for groups of friends who come for a cold beer and to appreciate the natural setting. The beach is visited by various eclectic groups in the evenings. Each of the kiosks attracts one of these different urban tribes, and it is considered courteous to find out which kiosk attracts which sort of person before sitting down.

Start at the **Ponta do Arpoador** (Arpoador Rock) **14**, where fishermen used to harpoon the whales that came to reproduce in the warm waters. Arpoador is the Portuguese for harpoon. Opposite the rock is the Arpoador muscle beach with fitness apparatus. From here you also get a good view back along Praia do Diabo and Arproador, the best surfing beach in Rio. Arpoador is clean, with nice sand and clear water – ideal for an early morning dip after utilising the exercise area.

*Arpoador, for clean sand and clear water*

There is a small path that starts halfway up the embankment overlooking the muscle beach. You have to scramble up the first few feet until you reach the official path, which is then clearly marked. At the top of the path is a skateboard area and a superb view of the beach. Follow a small path along the fence of the military area, and descend the long slope into **Parque Garota de Ipanema**. The park is the venue for some of the best free music around, with groups specialising in samba and *bossa nova* playing at weekends and holidays.

29

*Parque Garota de Ipanema*

Exit the park at the lower beach gate and turn right along the pedestrian walkway of Avenida Francisco Bhering towards the main area of Ipanema Beach. Enter the avenue along the seafront, making sure to look both ways at the cycle track that runs along the front all the way from Leblon to Parque do Flamengo and the city center.

You now enter Avenida Vieira Souto, and at No. 176 is **Casa de Cultura Laura Alvim** **15** (Monday to Friday 9am–10pm, Saturday and Sunday 4–10pm), with a colonial courtyard at the back which has been turned into a small cultural center for temporary exhibitions.

Turn into Rua Teixeira de Melo and walk one block inland to **Praça Gen. Osório** **16**, where on Sunday you will find the ★ **Feira Hippie** (Sunday 8am–7pm), Rio's Hippie Market with its 600 stands. Since 1966, Ipanema artists have sold their paintings, sculptures and music here, and, though now over 30 years old, the *feira* still has a fresh appeal. A famous modern sculpture fountain, *Chafariz das Saracuras*, is in the center.

*Feira Hippie in full swing*

The *praça* also has some excellent restaurants; if you want to try the traditional Brazilian dish of *feijoada*, black beans and pork, a specialist restaurant lies just off the square. **Casa da Feijoada** (*see page 80*) serves this dish accompanied by rice, *couve* (cabbage), fresh orange, *farofa de farinha de mandióca* and a traditional *caipirinha* alcoholic drink (*see page 77*).

*Garota de Ipanema for good food*

Walk back across the square, along Rua Prudente de Morais, until you get to the junction with Rua Vinícius de Moraes. Opposite you will find the restaurant★ **Garota de Ipanema** ⑰ (daily 11.30am–1am, *see page 80*), where the late Tom Jobim and Vinícius de Moraes used to sit and compose. A beautiful young girl named Helô Eneida Pinto (now Pinheiro) walked past every day on her way to the beach and inspired the song *The Girl from Ipanema*. She went on to become a top PR executive, earning a living from being 'The Girl', and the bar changed its name to the title of the song. It is stacked with memorabilia of the two famous composers and pictures of Helô. Although this is a tourist restaurant, the food is also better than average and not too expensive.

*Amsterdam Sauer creations*

Walk one more block inland and turn left on to Rua Visconde de Pirajá, one of the main shopping areas of Ipanema and Rio, with exclusive boutiques along this stretch for the next few blocks. At the junction with Rua Garcia d'Avila are the headquarters of two of the world's major jewelers, ★★ **Amsterdam Sauer** and **H. Stern** ⑱ (daily 9am–6pm), both of which have interesting exhibits. H. Stern runs a 12-minute tour of the factory facility with a special walkway behind glass so craftsmen can be seen working on the precious stones, and there is also a huge showroom of their work. Amsterdam Sauer has a museum, opened in 1989, which contains more than 3,000 dazzling specimens of cut and uncut gemstones that portray the country's vast wealth.

*Replica mine*

Make sure you see the alexandrite stone, one of the most valuable gems, which is named after Russian Czar Alexander II. It changes color from light green to deep red according to the light source. The world's biggest alexandrite, found in Bahia state in 1963, it weighs in at a massive 110,000 carats (22kg/48lb) and is featured in *The Guinness Book of Records*. The museum also has detailed replicas of two typical Brazilian mines. The tour and museum are free, and both companies will pick you up from hotels in the Zona Sul (Amsterdam Sauer tel: 239 8691, H. Stern tel: 259 7442).

From here continue walking along Rua Visconde de Pirajá. At the junction with Avenida Henrique Dumont is Praça Alcazar de Toledo with a modern art sculpture in the form of a yellow bridge over the road. This is not accessible to pedestrians as it is a folly only.

The next street on the left is Rua Paul Redfern, where you'll find one of the strangest sights in Rio. **The Lord**

**Jim Pub**  (6pm–last customer, *see page 80*) was owned for 16 years by Annie Philips, who built it as an authentic English pub. Annie is now at the Copacabana Palace and the Lord Jim has reopened under new management with some of the same staff, many of whom speak English. Further along, at the corner with Prudente de Morais, is a good selection of four restaurants and bars. In fact, Ipanema and Leblon are full of interesting restaurants and bars.

*Working out at Leblon*

Return to Rua Visconde de Pirajá and turn left to cross the canal which links the sea to Lagoa Rodrigo de Freitas and marks the boundary between Ipanema and **Leblon**. This region is named after Charles Leblon, a Frenchman who owned one of the largest farms in the area.

On the right is Jardim de Alah, on the left is Praça Alameda Saldanha Gama and straight ahead Avenida Ataulfo de Paiva, one of the most exclusive shopping streets in Rio. The **Rio Design Center** at No. 270 has designer shops showing the latest in Brazilian design for furniture and modern art. You can return to the seafront at any point along Avenida Ataulfo de Paiva and at the far end of Leblon Beach is the beginning of Avenida Niemeyer, which goes on along the coast to **São Conrado Beach**. From this elevated position at ★ **Mirante do Leblon**  you get a great view back along the beach.

*Baywatch Rio style*

**31**

A short distance along Avenida Niemeyer is the **Rio Sheraton Hotel** (*see page 95*) on **Vidigal Beach**, and further along is São Conrado (after the Sheraton you must take a bus), where the **Inter-Continental Hotel** and the exclusive **Gávea Golf Club** are located. **Rocinha**, Brazil's largest *favela* (shanty town, *see pages 12 and 90*), nestles on the hillside overlooking this expensive borough. At the end of São Conrado Beach is an area known as the **Praia do Pepino** which is used as a landing site for hang-gliders.

*Rocinha favela*

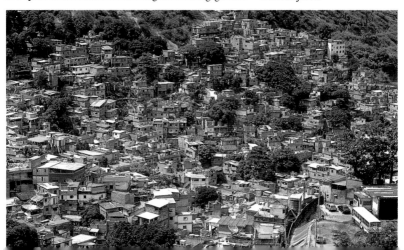

Refreshment for gardeners

Examining the flora

Aléia Barbosa Rodrigues, the
main avenue of Royal Palms

# Route 4

## The Gardens

### Jardim Botânico – Jockey Club – Lagoa Rodrigo de Freitas *See maps on pages 18–19 and opposite*

★★★ **Jardim Botânico ㉑**, the city's botanical gardens (buses 170, 524, 571, 572 or 594; daily 8am–5pm), offer the visitor a chance to see some of the more remarkable flora and fauna of Brazil and elsewhere. If you have not been to the tropics before, don't miss this real insight into the strange and wonderful plants that grow in these latitudes. It is recognized as the most important botanical garden in Latin America. With an area of 137 hectares (350 acres) and more than 6,500 species of flowers, 350,000 herbs, 6,100 fruits and 6,400 trees, it has been designated a Biosphere Reserve by UNESCO.

It all started in 1808 when Dom João (King of Portugal and Brazil from 1816 to 1831) decided to install a gunpowder factory in an old sugar mill. He acquired the mill and, inspired by his love for the place, had a garden planted next to the factory. This housed species brought from the East and, in the following year, Luiz Vieira da Silva, a naval officer, presented Dom João with avocado, litchi and cinnamon tree seedlings and an areca palm tree. They were planted in the garden and, to encourage the cultivation of new species, Dom João decided to offer rewards and duty exemptions to anyone who imported them for cultivation. In 1809 he planted a *Roystonea Oleracea*, brought from the Indian Ocean, which was the first of the Royal Palms to be cultivated in Brazil.

After Dom João had returned to Portugal, his son, Dom Pedro I, decided to open the gardens to the public. In 1824

Frei Leandro do Sacramento, the first botanical director, undertook important experiments and studies. Tea was grown on a large scale and it became a local craze for a time. Today the layout of the gardens still keeps the same basic design conceived by Frei Leandro and there is a pond he had built which bears his name.

Another botanical director, João Barbosa Rodrigues, was an internationally respected specialist in palms, rubber trees and orchids. During his administration, which started in 1890, the herbarium, the museum and the library (which contains 32,000 books) were inaugurated and the collection of plants considerably enlarged. He also constructed new buildings, greenhouses and the arboretum in the gardens. Because of his extensive work and great knowledge, Rodrigues is regarded as the person who did most for the park's reputation.

The bus stop for the Jardim Botânico is near the vehicle entrance **A**. You can enter here, as well as at the main entrance **B** just along the road.

First stop on a tour of the garden should be the **Visitors' Center C**, which is located in the old headquarters of the sugar mill. The mill was founded by Rio's governor, Antônio de Salema, in 1576, and later on was also used as a residence for the royal family while they were visiting the gardens. In 1989 fragments of pots in which the boiled syrup was placed until it solidified to become a 'sugar loaf' were found here; archeologists also unearthed stone objects from the Tamoios Indian village, which was destroyed when the mill was built.

The separate **cactus area D** is on the left of the Visitors' Center. Walk along the Aléia Pedro Gordilho

*Sculptures outside the Visitors' Center and bamboo in the Japanese Garden*

33

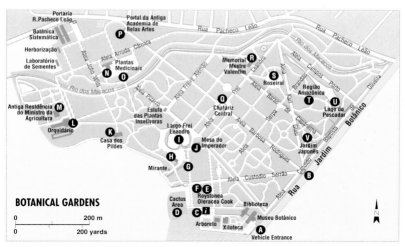

**BOTANICAL GARDENS**

0   200 m
0   200 yards

path, and on the right is the **Royal Palm** **E** that was planted by Dom João in 1809.

Next to this is the **Pau-Brasil** (Brazil Wood) area **F**. This was the first raw material to attract the interest of the Portuguese in Brazil. Growing up to 25m (80ft) high and 65cm (2ft) in diameter, with yellow flowers that have a pleasant perfume, the hardwood is heavy and has a dark red bark. It was the predominant wood of the Atlantic rainforest, but nowadays is rare in coastal areas.

*Giant water lilies at Largo Frei Leandro*

Just along Aléia Pedro Gordilho on the left is a region of pluvial (rainy) Atlantic secondary forest. The **small waterfall** **G** and artificial lakes were built to provide an environment for aquatic plants and distribute water to the garden. There is also a small grotto, **Gruta Karl Glasl** **H**, to accommodate species that like wet and humid rocks.

Continue to the **Largo Frei Leandro** **I**, also known as Largo das Vitórias Régias because of its giant water lilies. Slaves dug the lake (which contains carp), and the fountain, *Deusa Tétis* (Goddess Tetis), dates from 1862. To the right is a small mound with the **Mesa do Imperador** (Emperor's Table) **J** where Dom Pedro I would sit with his son.

*Orchid at the Orquidário*

Walk to the other side of the lake to **Casa dos Pilões** **K** (closed on Monday). Constructed in 1808, this was one of the seven gunpowder factory buildings. The most dangerous part of production, that of compacting the power, was carried out here. The building had a waterwheel which operated two bronze rams to pound the components together.

Turn left and walk along Aléia Alberto Loefgren to the **Orquidário** (Orchidarium) **L**. This is one of the great sights of the gardens with over 2,500 examples of 708 species of orchids. Don't miss the spectacular *Laelia Pumila* from Espírito Santos state, and *Oncidium Papilo*, with yellow and orange flowers, from Central America.

*Among the medicinal plants*

Turn left out of the Orquidário past what was the official residence of the **Minister of Agriculture** **M**. Walk to the Rio dos Macacos (River of Monkeys) and turn right along its bank. At Aléia John Wills take another left and cross the river to the area of **Plantas Medicinals** (medicinal plants) **N**. Next door is a gate, all that remains of this section of the old **gunpowder factory** **O**.

Turn left out of the gate and walk behind the children's playground, where the path emerges through some large bamboo trees at **Portal da Antiga Academia de Belas Artes** **P**. Built by Montigny, who was one of the French artists' mission of 1816, the fine arts academy was originally downtown, but with the modernization of the city, the arch was brought to the Botanical Gardens in the 1930s.

Now you join the main avenue of palms, **Aléia Barbosa Rodrigues**. The tallest were planted in 1842 and the smallest in 1951. Walk down the avenue to arrive at

Chafariz Central Ⓠ. Made in 1895 out of cast iron from England, the central fountain has two basins. In the center of the larger one are four feminine figures representing music, poetry, science and art.

Turn left at the fountain and walk along Frei Leandro. Continue until the **Memorial Mestre Valentim** Ⓡ. Valentim da Fonseca e Silva (1745–1813), the famous sculptor, created the work *Eco e Narciso*, which was the first sculpture to use cast iron in Brazil.

*'Eco e Narciso' sculpture*

Turn right for the **Roseiral** (rose garden) Ⓢ, and take a left and then right on to Aléia Campos Porto where the garden is covered by dense vegetation typical of the **Amazon Rainforest** Ⓣ. Look out for the *Pau Mulato* which has a shiny black bark that looks plastic in summer, but changes color according to the seasons.

At the end by the main road, turn right into Aléia Cândido Baptista de Oliveira, where there are exotic lotus flowers around the **Lago do Pescador** Ⓤ. Further along is the *Arecabambu* bamboo, which forms the basis for the **Jardim Japonês** (Japanese Garden) Ⓥ. The idea for this garden originated in 1935 when a Japanese economic mission donated 65 species of Japanese plants. In 1995 it was reopened in the presence of Princess Sayako, daughter of Emperor Akihito, to celebrate the centenary of the friendship treaty between Brazil and Japan.

**35**

*The Jockey Club from above*

Opposite the **Jardim Botânico** is the ★★ **Jóquei Clube** (Jockey Club) ㉒, one of the most beautiful race courses in the world. The view from the stands is magnificent and includes Corcovado and the statue of Christ (*see pages 20–23*). Racing in Rio dates back to 1825, but the present course was inaugurated in 1926. Races take place four times a week: Saturday and Sunday (from 2pm or 4 pm depending on the time of year); and Monday and Thursday night (from 4pm to 9.30pm, or 7pm to 11.30pm). The big race of the year, when a crowd of over 35,000 is common, is traditionally held the first Sunday in August.

*Lagoa Rodrigo de Freitas*

To the east of the Jockey Club, the **Lagoa Rodrigo de Freitas** has become a very popular recreation area, particularly at weekends. The lagoon is surrounded by three main park areas: Parque dos Patins and Parque das Taboas on the west side, and Parque do Cantagalo on the east. All three offer areas for volleyball, tennis, football and basketball, skating and cycling. A full circuit of the lagoon will take a fast cyclist about two hours, but there are 25 kiosks dotted around serving food and drink. On the lagoon itself you can hire rowing boats and pedaloes.

Opposite Parque do Cantagalo is Parque da Catacumba, with modern sculptures and forest trails built on land that used to be a *favela* (shanty town).

# Route 5

## Catete and Glória

**Museu da República – Museu do Folclore Edson Carneiro – Museu do Telefone – Castelinho – Hotel Glória – Igreja de Nossa Senhora da Glória do Outeiro – Parque do Flamengo – Enseada da Glória – Monumento Nacional aos Mortos da Segunda Guerra Mundial** *See map opposite*

Catete and Glória hold some of Rio's more important historical buildings. Both the magnificent Republic Museum, with its factual history of the Republican era, and the internationally renowned Folklore Museum illustrate how this area was once not only the seat of Brazilian government, but also an important center of culture in the post World War II era. Tucked away just a few hundred meters from the sea are some fascinating old museums and churches waiting to be explored, as well as the new developments along the seafront in Flamengo Park.

*Folkloric exhibits*

*Museu da República*

**★★ Museu da República ㉓** (Tuesday to Friday noon–5pm, Saturday and Sunday 2–6pm; free on Wednesday; guided tours available, tel: 265 9747) is next to Catete metro station. The Catete Palace in which the museum is housed was built between 1858 and 1867 for Antônio Clemente Pinto, a wealthy merchant and coffee planter, and represents the best remaining example of the colonial mansions in Rio.

The decline of the coffee plantations caused the palace to pass to several owners, but in 1896, during Prudente de Moraes' administration, the Federal Government bought it to install the presidency. From then, the palace housed 18 Brazilian presidents and numerous intense political negotiations took place within its walls, including the declarations of war against Germany in 1917 and 1942. Many major social affairs were also held here, and the palace witnessed the end of two presidents: the death of Alfonso Pena in 1909 and, in 1954, the suicide of President Getúlio Vargas; this was the result of a serious political and military crisis, and provoked waves of uncertainty throughout Brazil.

The last president to work here was Jucelino Kubitschek, who moved the capital and presidency to Brasília in 1960. Since then, the Catete Palace has been home to the Museu da República, which covers the political story of Brazil from the Proclamation of the Republic in 1889 until the capital's move.

*Artistic expressions*

On the ground floor are the entrance hall and the minister's room, which maintain the solemn atmosphere of the important political meetings and decisions made here. The other rooms on the ground floor house temporary exhibitions. The second story, known as the 'noble floor', has rooms with different themes, such as the Pompean, Moorish, Noble and Banquet Rooms. These contain masterpieces by Bernardelli, Batista da Costa, Gustavo Dall'Ara, Décio Villares and Rodolfo Amoedo. On the third floor a special exhibition shows many of the Republic's famous documents and memorabilia. President Vargas's private apartments are preserved, along with his blood-stained nightshirt and the bullet that killed him.

In the gardens (daily 8am–5.30pm) are a lake, grotto, fountain and bandstand where activities like music, plays, yoga and t'ai chi take place. There is also a theater, multimedia kiosk and educational center (Monday to Friday 9am–5pm, Saturday 2–6pm) with on-line access to the Internet that is much cheaper than in an Internet café.

Next to the palace is the ★★ **Museu do Folclore Edson Carneiro** (Folklore Museum) ㉔ (Tuesday to Friday 11am–6pm, Saturday and Sunday 3–6pm). The collection began in 1950 and has more than 12,000 objects representing lifestyles and artistic expressions of Brazil's different cultural groups, some priceless works of popular art. It offers an insight into the wide diversity of folklore, religious and cultural beliefs, from the *bumba-meu-boi* (typical folklore bull ceremony), to the production of *cachaça* alcohol (*see page 78*), along with Carnival costumes and masks.

Turn left out of the museum, walk along Rua do Catete for four blocks, then take another left into

ROUTE 5

0        250 m
0        250 yds

*Castelinho do Flamengo*

*Hotel Glória*

*Igreja de Nossa Senhora
da Glória do Outerio*

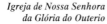

Rua Dois de Dezembro for the **Museu do Telefone** ㉕ (Tuesday to Sunday 9am–7pm). In 1918 a manual telephone exchange, with 2,597 lines belonging to the company Telefônica Beira-Mar, was installed in this building. It became an automatic exchange in 1930; some of the exhibits, however, go back to the very early days of telephones with examples and an explanation of modern telecommunications.

Continue down Rua Dois de Dezembro towards the sea, and on the corner with Praia do Flamengo is the **Castelinho do Flamengo, Centro Cultural Oduvaldo Vianna Filho** (Monday to Friday 2–8pm, Saturday and Sunday 4–8pm). Housed in what looks like a small castle this cultural center hosts photographic exhibitions, concerts and plays. Built by the architect Gino Copede in 1918, it synthesizes several European styles in its mainly eclectic design.

Cross Rua Dois de Dezembro, and walk along Praia do Flamengo, past the garden of the Catete Palace and the Manchete media group, to the ★ **Hotel Glória** ㉖, where you can wander in and take a look around one of Rio's oldest and grandest hotels (or perhaps even stay the night in the lap of luxury). Opened in 1922, it was Brazil's first reinforced-concrete building and the largest hotel in South America at the time.

Turn left out of the hotel, and you will see on a hill the ★★ **Igreja de Nossa Senhora da Glória do Outeiro** ㉗ (Monday to Friday 8am–noon, 1–5pm, Saturday and Sunday 8am–noon). In 1671 the hermit Antônio de Caminha constructed a small chapel dedicated to Nossa Senhora da Glória, which local history recalls was the most beautiful in Rio at that time.

Support grew for the religious group Nossa Senhora da Glória, and the present church was finished in 1739. Over the years the church became popular with Rio society and after the Portuguese royal family arrived in 1808, it became their favorite place of worship. It was traditional for the royal family to attend services here, although the official royal chapel was the Igreja de Nossa Senhora do Carmo da Antiga Sé (*see page 56*). The royal children were also christened here, one child bearing the name Maria da Glória (Maria II, Queen of Portugal), and in 1849 Dom Pedro II conferred the name 'Imperial' on the church's brotherhood, a title that was recognized by the Republic and continues to be respected today.

The interior of the octagonal church is richly decorated with ceramic tiles dating from 1735, with a monochromatic Baroque design showing biblical scenes. At the back is the **Museu da Imperial Irmandade de Nossa Senhora da Glória** (Tuesday to Friday 9am–noon and 1–5pm,

Saturday and Sunday 9am–noon). It houses a rich collection of documents and religious artefacts and jewelry, many of which have been donated by members of the royal family and Rio's nobility.

The museum also has a priceless oil painting by Felix Emílio Tauniy, depicting the miracle performed by Nossa Senhora da Glória when Dom Pedro's life was saved after falling from a horse in 1823. The Emperor is shown being held by an angel who is fencing with Death.

Make your way down into the square below the church on the right, where there is a huge **statue of São Sebastião**, the patron saint of Rio de Janeiro. His feast day is celebrated on 20 January.

*St Sebastian's Day procession*

To walk to the World War II memorial, cross the road near the traffic lights into **Parque do Flamengo**, sometimes referred to as Parque Brigadeiro Eduardo Gomes-Aterro. This is the biggest urban park in the world and full of family activities during the day. It is especially popular at weekends and holidays with local people, but after dark it is deserted and should be avoided. Known as the *aterro* (landfill) by residents, it is one of the most important landscaping projects designed by designer Roberto Burle Marx (*see page 74*). It includes museums, institutes, theaters, libraries, monuments and restaurants within its 120 hectares (297 acres).

**39**

Avenida Infante Dom Henrique, which cuts through the park, is an urban motorway, but is closed to traffic on Sunday. During the week use the footbridges to cross to the **Enseada da Glória**. This is Rio's main marina for yachts and boats, and craft of all sizes can be rented from here, as well as deep-sea fishing organized.

*Enseada da Glória*

Turn left and walk alongside the marina to the ★ **Monumento Nacional aos Mortos da Segunda Guerra Mundial** ⓳ (daily 9am–6pm). The monument honors 462 soldiers from the 25,000 strong Brazilian Expeditionary Force who were killed in Italy, as well as all those who lost their lives in World War II. The museum displays uniforms, decorations, equipment and arms from Brazil, USA and Germany, which were used in the conflict.

*Monument to the fallen*

Above the museum is the giant concrete structure of the Tomb of the Unknown Soldier where there is an eternal flame. It was built between 1957 and 1960, and on the first Sunday of the month one of the three forces, in turn, carries out a changing of the guard ceremony at 10am. The monument itself represents two arms raised with the hands 'outstretched beseeching God in prayer'. In 1980, Pope John Paul II celebrated mass from the steps for a crowd of more than two million people.

A short walk across the park from the monument brings you to the **Museu de Arte Moderna** and start of Route 6.

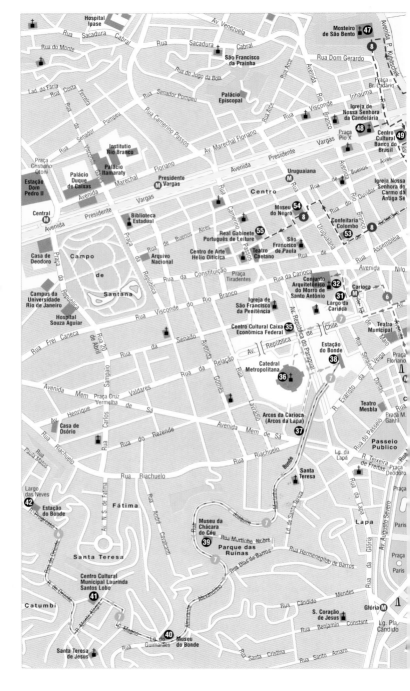

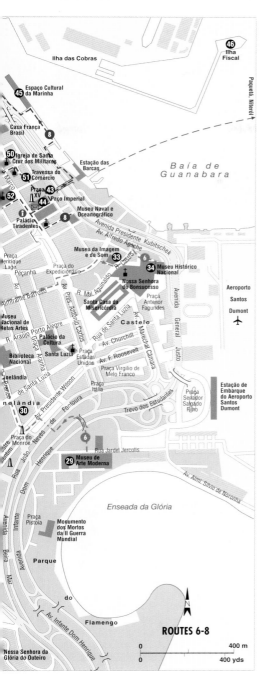

Ilha das Cobras

Ilha Fiscal 46

Paquetá, Niterói

Espaço Cultural da Marinha 45

Casa França Brasil 3

Igreja de Santa Cruz dos Militares 50

Estação das Barcas

Baía de Guanabara

Travessa do Comércio 51

Praça XV 43

Paço Imperial 44

52

Palácio Tiradentes

Museu Naval e Oceanográfico

8

Avenida Presidente Kubitschek
Av. Alfredo Agache

Praça Henrique Lage
Peçanha

Praça do Expedicionário

Museu da Imagem e do Som 33

R. Castro

Museu Histórico Nacional 34

Nossa Senhora do Bonsucesso

Almirante Barroso

Av. Pres. Antônio Carlos

Santa Casa da Misericórdia

Rua de Santa Luzia

R. Mal. Aguinaldo

Castelo

Praça Antenor Fagundes

Aeroporto Santos Dumont

Museu Nacional de Belas Artes

R. Araújo Porto Alegre

Graça Aranha

Palácio da Cultura

Santa Luzia

Biblioteca Nacional

Praça Estados Unidos

Av. Churchill

Av. F. Roosevelt

Praça Virgílio de Melo Franco

Praça Senador Salgado Filho

Estação de Embarque do Aeroporto Santos Dumont

inelândia

de Santa Luzia

Praça Itália

Marechal Câmara

General Justo

nelândia 30

Av. Presidente Wilson

Fontoura

Trevo dos Estudantes

Praça do Monroe

Praça João Neves de

Rua Jardel Jercolis

6

Museu de Arte Moderna 29

Av. Almte. Silvio de Noronha

Rua João Henrique

Dom

Enseada da Glória

Praça Pistoia

Monumento dos Mortos da II Guerra Mundial

Avenida Infante

Beira Mar

Parque

do

Flamengo

N

ROUTES 6-8

Nossa Senhora da Glória do Outeiro

Av. Infante Dom Henrique

0          400 m
0          400 yds

*Natural History Museum p46*

41

*Santa Teresa trams p48–9*

001

*Praça Floriano*

# Route 6

The City Center: Across the Centuries

Museu de Arte Moderna – Aeroporto Santos Dumont – Cinelândia – Biblioteca Nacional – Museu Nacional de Belas Artes – Praça Floriano – Teatro Municipal – Largo da Carioca – Conjunto Arquitetônico do Morro de Santo Antônio – Igreja da Ordem Terceira de São Francisco da Penitência – Museu da Imagem e do Som – Museu Histórico Nacional *See map on pages 40–41*

This route incorporates some of Rio's important modern buildings, including the Museum of Modern Art, as well as the historic downtown district known as Cinelândia with its museums and galleries. Continuing along Rio's main avenue, once considered the Champs Elysées of Brazil, to Largo da Carioca, one of the original squares from where the churches that make up the Conjunto Arquitetônico do Morro de Santo Antônio overlook the modern city center. The journey ends at the National History Museum, which, apart from being a significant historical building, is packed with fascinating artefacts and displays.

*Museu de Arte Moderna*

Opened in 1958, the ★ **Museu de Arte Moderna** (Modern Art Museum) ㉙ (Tuesday to Sunday noon–6pm) is located at the north end of Parque do Flamengo. Locals think it looks like an aircraft hangar, perhaps due to its proximity to the airfield, but it has attracted important works of art, including a collection of Brazilian modern art donated by Gilberto Chateaubriand. It also houses work by Di Cavalcanti, Portinari and Anita Malfati and is considered the most important modern art museum in Latin

America. There is an extensive library, one of the most important film and movie poster archives in Latin America, an art workshop area, and a restaurant on the ground floor surrounded by modern art.

From the museum you can look and walk (via the parking area) across to **Aeroporto Santos Dumont** (with easy access from Galeão International Airport and on bus routes from most places). Alberto Santos Dumont, for whom the airport is named, was an aviation pioneer. In 1899, four years before Wilbur and Orville Wright flew a heavier-than-air machine, he piloted a dirigible that circled the Eiffel Tower in Paris, and returned to the Aero Club of France, taking 29.5 minutes to cover the 11-km (7-mile) trip.

*Aeroporto Santos Dumont*

He also invented the first airplane to take off, land and take off again unaided. Until his '14 Bis' airplanes, flown in Paris in 1906, aircraft had used devices such as catapults to get airborne. He had Cartier design a watch that could be strapped to his wrist, thus inventing the wristwatch. He is a Brazilian legend, and Brazilians feel let down that the world remembers the Wright brothers and does not give Santos Dumont his due recognition. When President Bill Clinton visited Brazil, he paid homage to Santos Dumont as the true inventor of the airplane.

**43**

The airport, which serves short-haul domestic flights and most importantly the shuttle service between Rio and São Paulo, stands on land that once belonged to the Calabouço Prison (*see page 46*).

To continue the walk return to the Museu de Arte Moderna and use the pedestrian bridge to cross the busy road that runs through the park. At Avenida Beira Mar turn left and head up towards the major crossroads with Avenida Rio Branco; to your right, as you cross Praca 4 de Julho, you can see the US Consulate (the US Embassy prior to the capital's move to Brasília). At Avenida Rio Branco don't cross, but head up on the right-hand side towards **Cinelândia** , an area so named in the 1930s because the city's main cinemas were all here. Many still survive. Notice, on your left, the *Chafariz do Monroe* fountain in Praça Mahatma Gandhi, and behind it the Passeio Público, the oldest park in Rio. The sea used to come right up to the gates before the Flamengo Park landfill project.

*Cinelândia:*
*Teatro Municipal detail*

To the right, as you walk up Avenida Rio Branco, is the **Biblioteca Nacional** (National Library, Monday to Friday 9am–8pm, Saturday 9am–3pm), the sixth-largest library in the world and the biggest in Latin America. Built in 1905, it has over three million books, including the collection Dom João brought from Portugal in 1808. He founded the Royal Library in 1810 and, in 1814, with 60,000 books, it was the first library to open to the public.

*The National Library*

The rarest items in the present collection are the *Os Lusíadas* first edition of 1572 by the Portuguese poet Luís de Camões, the *Bible of Mogúnci* of 1462, and 122 engravings by Albrecht Dürer (1471–1528).

Just beyond the library is the ★★ **Museu Nacional de Belas Artes** (Tuesday to Friday 10am–6pm, Saturday and Sunday 2–6pm). It was built in 1908 for the Academy of Fine Arts which was originally founded when the French artistic mission of 1816 arrived in Brazil to arrange the official teaching of art – the reason why the building resembles the Paris Louvre. It became a museum in 1937, and now houses 20,000 objects of art including painting, sculpture, engravings and 54 works by Joaquim Lebreton who was in charge of the French mission. It is considered by many to be the city's most important permanent art collection.

*Museu Nacional de Belas Artes*

In the Eliseu Visconti gallery are works by famous Brazilian artists including some by Anita Malfati, Di Cavalcanti, Lasar Segall and Cícero Dial. The third-floor area, dedicated to foreign artists, contains 20 paintings by the pre-Impressionist Boudin (1824–98). There are also permanent exhibitions of indigenous art, African art, and ceramics.

Across Avenida Rio Branco from the museum is Praça Floriano which houses the **Palácio Pedro Ernesto** (City Hall) built in 1923 (open while in session). If you visit, note that shorts are not allowed to be worn in government buildings.

*Teatro Municipal*

**44**

At the top of Praça Floriano is the ★ **Teatro Municipal** (tel: 286 3234), a small-scale replica of the Paris Opera. Opened in 1909, and at the time the city's most expensive and luxurious building, it has since hosted many international stars of opera, ballet, theater and music.

In the basement, and accessed from Avenida Rio Branco, is the **Café do Teatro**, decorated with huge ceramic tableaux of Persian themes. The foyer contains a tiled tableau of Molière's *Le Bourgeois Gentilhomme*. Facing the theater is the statue of the composer and conductor Carlos Gomes (1836–96), who wrote a famous Brazilian opera, *O Guarani*, based on the history of the Guarani Indians.

*Largo da Carioca*

Continue up Avenida Rio Branco to the metro station Carioca, and cut through to your left to **Largo da Carioca** ③①. Above, on a small hill, is the ★★★ **Conjunto Arquitetônico do Morro de Santo Antônio** ③②. This comprises the **Igreja e Convento de Santo Antônio** (normally Monday to Friday 7.30am–6.30pm, Saturday 7.30am–11.30am and 2.30–6pm, Sunday 9.30am–11.30am), and the **Igreja da Ordem Terceira da São Francisco da Penitência** (tel: 262 0197 to confirm times and access for both churches

due to restoration work). Cut into the rock is a small tunnel leading to an elevator.

*Conjunto Arquitetônico do Morro de Santo Antônio*

The convent was completed in 1616, but because of overcrowding another was constructed in 1780. During the French invasion of 1710, Rio's inhabitants hid in the church, thus ensuring a good relationship between the religious order and the population.

**45**

Completed in 1620, the church has a neo-colonial facade with a simple architectural structure and one nave without a lateral chapel. The interior is baroque and the church bells are housed in the roof of the convent. The 18th-century German organ has six angels supporting the major pipework, all of which is above the main door. Make sure you see the wood and leather bust, sculpted in Japan in 1597, depicting the 18 Franciscan martyrs who died there. The sacristy is considered the most beautiful in Rio, with its painted ceiling showing the history of St Anthony.

*St Anthony of Padua inside the church*

Igreja da Orderm Terceira da São Francisco da Penitência was finished in 1737. On the ceiling is the first perspective painting in Brazil, symbolizing the divinity of San Francisco, which was executed over three years by Caetano da Costa Coelho. The baroque carvings are said to be the best of their type in Latin America. In one of the ante rooms, on the way to the sacristy, are oil paintings of Dom Pedro II and Teresa Cristina.

Between these two churches is the original 1622 chapel of the Nossa Senhora da Conceição order, still with much of the gold carving. Prince Dom Juan Carlos of Spain, the son-in-law of Dom João VI, was buried here in 1812.

Descend in the elevator and return to Largo da Carioca. Here you can now either complete Route 6 with the two museums below, or take Route 7 with a tram trip through historic Santa Teresa, returning later to finish this route.

Now, or later when you finish Route 7, cross Avenida Rio Branco and walk down Avenida Almirante Barroso.

After four blocks cross Avenida Presidente Antônio Carlos and walk to the far side of Praça do Expedicionário.

On the right is the hospital Santa Casa da Misericórdia, and at the far side, to your right, is the **Museu da Imagem e do Som** (Museum of Image and Sound) ㉝ (Monday to Friday 1–6pm). Built to commemorate the first century of Brazil's independence, it houses a collection of popular national music and recorded interviews with important artists and politicians. There is also a large collection of photographs of old Rio de Janeiro.

*Museo Histórico Nacional*

Behind lies Praça Marechal Âncora. Walk towards the elevated road at the far side and turn right to to arrive at the entrance to the ★★ **Museo Histórico Nacional** (National History Museum) ㉞ (Tuesday to Friday 10am–5.30pm, Saturday and Sunday 2–6pm). Built in 1603 as a fort, Fortaleza de São Tiago, it then became the Calabouço Prison in 1693 and a Royal Arsenal in 1822. The building was completely transformed in 1922 when an international exhibition was held here to celebrate the first 100 years of Brazil's independence. Since then it has been the National History Museum and is probably the most important historical museum in Brazil. It has the largest collection in Latin America of coins, banknotes and old cannons and, in covering the history of Brazil from its discovery in 1500 to the Proclamation of the Republic in 1889, complements the more recent artefacts at the Museu da República (*see Route 5, pages 36–7*).

In the National History Museum make sure that you see the homeopathic pharmacy display, removed from a local shop, which was in use from 1847 until 1983. Also the giant painting *Batalha do Riachuelo* by Vitor Meireles is well worth a look, as well as the painting of the last *Royal Ball on Ilha Fiscal* by Aurélio de Figueiredo e Melo.

*In the galleries*

# Route 7

Santa Teresa

**Centro Cultural Caixa Económica Federal – Catedral Metropolitana – Arcos da Carioca – Tram Museum and ride – Santa Teresa District – Parque das Ruínas – Museu Chácara do Céu – Largo do Guimarães – Museu do Bonde – Centro Cultural Laurinda Santos Lobos – Casa Jimmy – Largo das Neves** *See map on pages 40–41*

The district of Santa Teresa grew around the Convent of Santa Teresa, just outside the old city center. In the 18th century runaway slaves and criminals hid in the forests that covered the hillsides of the borough. The River Carioca was used as a water supply for the city center, and its canalization was not popular with residents who owned small farms so they started to move further in to the Zona Sul. Santa Teresa then went through a period of decay, but never lost its feeling of tranquility and freshness which contrasted with the neighboring business area. In recent decades it has been rediscovered and colonized by artists, who hold studio events open to the public. The tram, from downtown Rio, takes its passengers near an old ruined mansion, now rebuilt as a cultural center, and on to one of Rio's famous art museums. In the center of Santa Teresa, it is possible to learn about the history of the tram and take another tram further into the labyrinth of narrow streets to the local museum and library. You can also visit a street kids' shelter project before ending up at a lovely little town square and returning by tram to the center.

*Bar do Albio, Santa Teresa*

**47**

From Metro Carioca or Largo da Carioca turn right along Avenida República de Chile. The building on the left, which looks like a Rubik cube, is the headquarters of Petrobrás, the Brazilian Petroleum Company. At the next corner is the **Centro Cultural Caixa Econômica Federal ㉟** (Monday to Friday 10am–6.30pm), which has a gallery with a collection of 300 paintings and sculptures by artists such as Tarsila do Amaral, Portinari, Di Cavalcanti and an entire wall carved in wood by Poty. It also houses temporary exhibitions, has a museum and library, and the popular Teatro Nelson Rodrigues.

Opposite is the **★★ Catedral Metropolitana ㊱** (Monday to Saturday 7am–6pm, Sunday 9am–6pm). The foundation stone was laid in 1964, and it was inaugurated in 1976. It is a huge concrete cone with a diameter of 106m (348ft) and 83m (272ft) high, and the main door, or Portal of Faith, has 48 bronze reliefs. It can accommodate 20,000, as it did when Pope John Paul II visited in 1980,

*Catedral Metropolitana inside and out*

and has a single granite stone weighing 8.5 tonnes as its altar. Suspended above the altar is a 10m (33ft) cross, and beneath the floor is a crypt with a capacity for the remains of 26,000 bodies.

*Arcos da Carioca*

If you want to see the ★ **Arcos da Carioca** ㊲, also known as Arcos da Lapa, from ground level pass around the back of the cathedral and underneath the arches. When constructed in 1750, in the style of a Roman aqueduct, it was the most complex structure in Latin America with 42 separate arches stretching 330m (1,803ft). Built with Brazilian granite to bring water from the River Carioca into the center of the city, since 1896 it has been used as a bridge by the Santa Teresa tram. The square below the arches is a natural amphitheater and hosts many events.

Return by the same route, and cross Avenida República do Paraguai from the cathedral side, to the ★★★ **Estação de Bondes** ㊳ for a tram ride through Santa Teresa. This district was once the scene for many leftist movements in Rio and a place of rest and inspiration for artists. The tram, the architecture, the peaceful streets, the fresh air all give the impression of traveling back in time. Take any tram (departures every 15 minutes) to the first stop (station with a central platform) named Curvelo and walk down Rua Dias de Barros.

*Parque das Ruinas*

Turn left into Rua Murtinho Nobre (five minutes' walk) to **Parque das Ruínas** (daily 10am–5pm and Thursday 10am–10pm; tel: 252 0112 or 252 1039 for details of events), an old ruined mansion that has been partly restored to provide a unique style of space for a cultural center. In the 1920s all the famous Brazilian figures of the time visited the house of Laurinda Santos Lobo, nicknamed the 'marshal of elegance', and the house was famous for her parties. With the death of the owner in 1946, the mansion fell into decay, only being saved from total destruction by the local council in 1997. At the top of the house is a look-out over the city, with a spectacular 360-degree view back to the cathedral, and towards the Santos Dumont airport and Sugar Loaf.

*Museu Chácara do Céu*

Walk further up Rua Murtinho Nobre to ★ **Museu Chácara do Céu** ㊴ (daily, except Tuesday, noon–5pm). The famous connoisseur and art collector Castro Maya lived here until his death in 1968, and his mansion, 'The Little Villa in the Sky' built in 1957, houses a large collection of art including works by Di Cavalcanti, Portinari, Monet, Picasso, Matisse and Salvador Dalí. The gardens, which were designed by Burle Marx (*see page 74*), offer a superb view of Guanabara Bay and downtown Rio.

Return to the tram by the same route and take the service to **Museu do Bonde** (Tram Museum) ㊵ (Rua Carlos Brandt 14, 9am–4.30pm). Get off at Largo do Guimarães, and the museum is in on your right. Founded in 1979, and originally at the main city terminus, it moved to this location in 1999 as part of the project to revitalize the tram system, which had gained a bad reputation. Passengers used to be able to jump on to the trams at any time, and cling to the sides without paying, which led to a spate of robberies. The line has now been restructured making it more secure and the police ride on many of the trams, certainly as far as the tram museum. However, still be careful and do not hang out of the side with a camera over your shoulder. The museum has around 300 items illustrating the history of the trams in Rio.

*Tram museum exhibit*

This area is in the heart of Santa Teresa with several good restaurants and bars. Try Bar do Arnaudo (Rua Almirante Alexandrina 316) for dishes from the Brazilian northeast, or Adega do Pimenta (Rua Almirante Alexandrina 296) for German food.

From Largo do Guimarães take a tram to Paula Matos, which takes the right-hand track and ends up at Largo das Neves. When the tram makes a sharp left turn into Rua Monte Alegre ask to be let off, and immediately on the right is **Centro Cultural Municipal Laurinda Santos Lobo** ➍ (Tuesday to Friday 10am–6pm, Saturday and Sunday 2–6pm; tel: 242 9741 for details of events). It was built in 1907 for Baronesa Parina, with a marble staircase leading to the upper terrace where the main wall of the building is covered with fine Italian flowered tiles. Under later owners a huge fish pond, surrounded by ceramic statues and a stage, where music groups performed during garden parties, were added. The council acquired the house in the late 1970s, and in 1995 a grant allowed the conversion into a cultural center with music performances, videos, lectures and workshops. A permanent exhibition about Santa Teresa is housed here, plus a public library.

One of the best-known residents of Rua Monte Alegre is the 'Great Train Robber' Ronald Biggs, who can often be seen out and about in the local shops and restaurants.

*Casa Jimmy*

The tram will stop for you again if you hail the driver. Continue on towards Largo das Neves for **Casa Jimmy** (tel: 507 5452 for an appointment). This started as a British-sponsored project to help young children who would have otherwise become street kids. It now receives help from the city, and is open to visitors who are interested in learning more about the problems faced by young abandoned children in Rio. Be prepared to make a donation.

Catch the tram, or walk, down Rua do Oriente to **Largo das Neves** ➋, a lovely little square, and soak up some of the local atmosphere at Bar do Abílio while you await the arrival of the next tram to take you back.

*Royal barge in the Espaço Cultural da Marinha*

# Route 8

## The Historic Center

**Praça XV – Paço Imperial – Espaço Cultural da Marinha – Mosteiro de São Bento – Igreja de Nossa Senhora da Candelária – Centro Cultural Banco do Brasil – Igreja de Santa Cruz dos Militares – Travessa do Comércio – Igreja de N.S. do Carmo da Antiga Sé – Igreja da Ordem Terceira de N.S. do Carmo – Confeitaria Colombo – Museu do Negro – Real Gabinete Português de Leitura** *See map on pages 40–41*

Starting at the heart of the old city of Rio, in Praça XV, where the royal family first landed and lived, this route demonstrates how and why Rio came into existence. Visiting one of Brazil's most ornate churches, Mosteiro de São Bento, the walk takes in the old trading centers of the Bank of Brazil and the French cultural center, which used to be a customs house. After visiting the old post office headquarters and a military church, it explores the twisting lanes around Travessa do Comércio, giving a taste of this quaint area where Rio's main commerce thrived in colonial times. There is also the opportunity to view the city's last remaining oratorio statue and relive the *belle époque* era by having afternoon tea at the beautifully appointed Colombo tea rooms.

*Praca XV*

★★ **Praça XV ⓭** (buses 119, 154, 413, 415, 455, 472) lies at the heart of the old city. In 1590, when the area was a sandy stretch of coast, the Carmelite Fathers built a convent here. In 1700 the Royal Warehouses were built, and later expanded with a mansion for the governor in the 1740s. When the Portuguese royal family arrived, after fleeing from Napoleon, the Viceroy's Mansion, as it was known, was transformed into a royal palace and subsequently became known as the Imperial Palace (Paço Imperial).

The square saw not only the arrival of the Portuguese royal family in 1808, but also its departure for exile 81 years later, after Brazil had been declared a republic on 15 November 1889. To commemorate the event the square was renamed Praça XV.

The ★ **Paço Imperial** ⓭ (Tuesday to Sunday noon–6.30pm), built in 1743, was only a temporary home of the Portuguese royal family when they first arrived in Rio. Dom João didn't like the palace, so they moved to what is now the National Museum (*see page 58*). From this building Dom Pedro II declared his Dia do Fico, when he disobeyed orders from Portugal and announced he would stay in Brazil, and Princesa Isabel signed the Lei Áurea abolishing slavery in Brazil in 1888. Until the end of the 19th century the palace was the Brazilian empire's seat of government. Restored in 1984, today it houses a Culture and Art Center.

*Paço Imperial*

Also in the square is the *Chafariz do Mestre Valentim* fountain. Constructed in 1789, it brought clean water into the city center from the River Carioca. However, the fountain you see today replaced an earlier one, erected around 1750, which stood where the statue of Marechal Manuel Luíz Osório now stands. Valentim da Fonseca e Silva, a famous sculptor, won the contract to repair and relocate the old fountain, but found it had deteriorated so much that he proposed the building of a new one. Today the fountain is hailed as one of the most important surviving pieces from Brazil's colonial time.

*Colonial fountain*

**51**

On the waterfront is the ferry station with boats to Niterói and other places in the Guanabara Bay area. As you stand facing the station, on your left is a tall, white building with a frieze of men fishing above the main doors. Take the small walkway under the flyover on the left of the building. As you pass along this walkway notice the old fish market stalls inside the basement.

Just past the building turn right into the ★ **Espaço Cultural da Marinha** (Naval Cultural Center) ⓮ (Tuesday to Friday noon– 5.30pm, Saturday and Sunday 9am– 5.30pm). Run by the Brazilian Navy, the center has displays of maritime history, including the royal barge used by Dom João VI. As well as explanations of early maritime navigation, including a copy of the world's oldest naval chart, there is also a section devoted to sub-aquatic archaeology dealing with finds from 1648 to 1916. Another section shows models of different types of boats in Brazil, from hollowed-out tree trunks used by Indians to

*Naval days recreated*

Amazon River boats. A submarine, employed by Brazil in World War II to escort merchant shipping, floats alongside the dock and can be visited.

*Ilha Fiscal clock tower*

★★ **Ilha Fiscal** (Customs Island) **⑯** (access by boat organized by the museum, tel: 233 9165 for up-to-date timetable) can also be visited, having recently been opened to the public for the first time in over 100 years. The building, which is an island, was constructed as a customs house in 1881, but the original design was changed from simply functional to a beautiful Gothic style after Dom Pedro II visited and fell in love with the views of Guanabara Bay. It was finished in 1889, just in time for the last big Imperial Ball held here only six days before the downfall of the monarchy when the military seized power under Marechal Manuel Deodoro da Fonseca. The ball was a big affair with 3,000 guests, and it took 80 chefs five days to prepare the food.

The island has permanent exhibitions about the work of the navy in the Amazon and Pantanal, and the oceanography of the bay area.

Turn right out of the marina gates and follow the elevated section of road. Eventually you will see a building with two giant cannons outside. This is the Arsenal de Marinha, unfortunately not open to the public. Turn right into Rua 1 de Março, and at the far end are the steps leading up to

*Mosteiro de São Bento*

★★★ **Mosteiro de São Bento** **⑰** (Monday to Friday 7am–11am and 2.30–6pm, Saturday 7.15am–6pm, Sunday 8.15am–6pm; mass Monday to Friday 3pm and 5pm, Sunday 10am). If the gates are not open walk along Rua Dom Geraldo to the traffic entrance or take the elevator hidden in No. 40.

The Benedictine monks living here divide the hours between work and prayer. The sacristy, cloister and living accommodation of the monks are private, but the church is open to visitors. Founded in 1590, for 200 years it received donations and grants that enabled it to purchase land and become self-sufficient. The present church was dedicated in 1641, having taken eight years to build with help from the slaves who worked in the monastery's sugar mill and on its lands.

*The monastery doors*

The main cast-iron gates were made in England and fitted in 1880. The inner wooden doors were made from clove and cinnamon with jacaranda and mahogany pieces in 1671. In the center between the 'false chapels' is a windbreaker made in 1736, showing episodes from the life of St Benedict.

All the main side chapels were paid for by 'brotherhoods' or 'confraternities', which were important in the colonial period. When the first side chapel, dedicated to St Christopher in 1673, was being constructed, the Abbot had a clause inserted in the deed that the wealthy patrons had to decorate the chapel and provide silver ornaments. This clause has been repeated for every side chapel since, ensuring that this is one of the most highly decorated churches in Brazil.

The only 'confraternity' still in existence is that of St Blaise, whose deeds refer to 'the brown men named below'. These brown, or *mulatto*, men were liberated slaves or slave descendants, most of whom were goldsmiths. A special mass is still celebrated each year for this group (first side chapel on right). This chapel, along with the next two, St Gertrude's and St Lawrence's, were covered with whitewash, and the original paintings only discovered during restoration work in 1976. The next on the right is Our Lady of Conception's chapel, and at one time the church carried her name.

Across the body of the church, nearest to the entrance, is the chapel of St Cajetan, who was a preacher who demanded absolute poverty from his followers. Next is the chapel of Our Lady of Pillar, paid for by a brotherhood so wealthy that it contributed funds for the ransom of the city during the French invasion of 1711. Third on the left is St Maur's chapel, and next is the Blessed Sacrament chapel, the first to be created, but then known as St Christopher's chapel, whose statue is now in the Baptistry. The candelabrum is from the original chapel, which was enlarged in 1800.

In the main body of the church the large silver candelabra were finished in 1795, and they light the gilded carved altar, walls and arch, dating from the 1780s. The painted ceilings are by Fra Ricardo do Pilar, completed in 1680. The ancient carvings date from 1670, but were gilded about 40 years later. The bars that separate the side chapels from the main body of the church originally separated the faithful from the priests celebrating mass, and are carved in jacaranda wood. An organ has been here since 1652, but an electric one was installed in 1945.

There are 12 statues representing Saints of the Benedictine Order. St Benedict is portrayed as a beardless young abbot in a statue on one side of the main altar, and St Scholástica, his twin sister, on the other side, is seen holding a book representing the Order. Above them, in the center, is the main altar statue of Our Lady of Montserrat.

Return to Rua 1 de Março and walk south. On the right are Avenida Marechal Floriano and Avenida Presidente Vargas. About 1.5km (1 mile) along Avenida Marechal Floriano is the **Itamaraty Palace**, home to the Brazilian Foreign Office from 1889 until its move to Brasília in 1970. Dating from 1854, the building, which today is a diplomatic museum, was home to the first Brazilian

*The nave lit by candelabra*

*The old organ*

presents (1889–97) but its most distinguished resident was the Barão do Rio Branco, Brazil's foreign minister who helped shape South America as it is known today.

At the intersection of Avenida Presidente Vargas and Rua 1 de Março is **Igreja de Nossa Senhora da Candelária ⑱** (Monday to Friday 7.30am–noon 1–4.30pm; Sunday 8am–1pm). It was constructed in 1634 in gratitude by a naval commandant who was protected during a storm after praying to Nossa Senhora da Candelária. Later, in 1755, a new church was erected on the site. Completed in 1811, the cupola, made from Lioz stone in a neoclassical style, was imported from Lisbon, and many people at the time thought the foundations would not support its 630 tonnes.

*Church built in gratitude*

Carrying on along Rua 1 de Março to the ★ **Centro Cultural Banco do Brasil ⑲** (Tuesday to Sunday noon–8pm). Built in 1880 this neo-classical style building became the headquarters of the Banco do Brasil in 1920, and remained the symbol of Brazil's financial world until 1960 when it became a branch office. In the late-1980s, the bank decided to rescue the building's symbolic and architectural worth. It is now a center for cultural activities. As well as four superb galleries for temporary exhibitions there is a theater, cinema, video room and public library. The historical archive, on the first floor, houses the bank's permanent exhibition of banknotes and coins, which trace the country's political and economic development. There is a wood-paneled tea room on the second floor, and a good view of the building's domed roof from the balcony outside it.

*Centro Cultural Banco do Brasil*

Behind Centro Cultural Banco do Brasil is the old customs house, **Casa França Brasil** (Tuesday to Sunday noon–5.30pm), which was actually built to be the Praça do Comércio (Commercial Place). When the French artists arrived in 1816 they brought the neoclassical style with them. This is the only public building in Rio de Janeiro dating from that time that has not been modernized. It remained the customs house until 1944, but is now a center for cultural exchange between France and Brazil.

*Centro Cultural dos Correios*

Walk between the Casa França Brasil and the Banco do Brasil along Rua Visconde de Itaboraí to the **Centro Cultural dos Correios** (Tuesday to Friday 10am–7pm, Saturday 8am–noon). This *eclético*-style building was constructed at the turn of the 20th century as a school but was also the office of the director of the post office. It now houses exhibitions of painting, photography and sculpture. The ride to the second floor in the original cage elevator is nostalgic, and the center has a good café.

Take the small street opposite, Travessa Tocantins, back to Rua 1 de Março, and turn left past the Central Post

Office. On the next block is **Igreja de Santa Cruz dos Militares** ⑩ (Monday to Friday 1.30–3.30pm; mass Monday, Wednesday, Friday and Saturday noon). In 1623 the Santa Cruz Fort stood here by the sea, but the fort started to fall apart, so the military asked if they could erect a temple to bury their dead. The temple was built in 1628 and, after several rebuilds and a big fire in 1914, the present church was constructed on the site.

At the side of this church is **Rua do Ouvidor,** one of the most exclusive streets in Rio in the 16th century. It became the first pedestrian street in the city in 1829, and the first to be illuminated by gas in 1854.

On the corner of Rua do Ouvidor and Travessa do Comércio is **Igreja de Nossa Senhora da Lapa dos Mercadores**, originating from a public oratorio built by traveling salesmen who were devoted to Nossa Senhora da Lapa. Construction started in 1747 after rich merchants put up money to buy the land.

Walk along **Travessa do Comércio** ⑤ to the Arco Imperial Restaurante e Churrascaria (*see page 78*). This is the site of the guest house of Dona Maria, the mother of the internationally famous Brazilian singer and actress, Carmen Miranda. The restaurant doesn't make much out of the fact that someone so famous once stayed here, but upstairs it has some interesting paintings showing views of old Rio.

At the end of Travessa do Comércio is the **Arco do Teles,** which forms part of what was a very exclusive house built for Francisco Teles de Menezes, the judge who specialized in dealing with the orphans of Rio in the 18th century. The last colonial arch to survive in Rio, it forms a passage from Travessa do Comércio, and connects Rua do Ouvidor and Praça XV.

Continue along the Praça XV side of Rua 1 de Março. Next door to the Paço Imperial is **Palácio Tiradentes**

*Bar on Travessa do Comércio*

55

*Igreja de Nossa Senhora da Lapa dos Mercadores*

*Palácio Tiradentes*

(Tuesday to Friday 10am–7pm, Saturday 10am–6pm, Sunday noon–5pm; shorts must not be worn in government buildings). Built in 1926, it is an impressive example of the architectonic eclecticism of the Cariocan *belle epóque*, and an important building in Brazilian contemporary history. It functioned in various political forms until the capital was transferred to Brasília. In 1975, when the new state of Rio de Janeiro was formed, it became the Legislative Assembly. The 4.5m (15ft) bronze statue outside is of Tiradentes, the martyr of the Inconfidência Mineira movement, who was imprisoned in a jail on this site in 1792, after which he was hung and quartered and his remains returned to Minas Gerais.

*Museu Naval e Oceanográfico*

Behind the palace, in Rua Dom Manoel, is the **Museu Naval e Oceanográfico** (daily noon–4.45pm). Housed in the old Naval Club, it has the original letter written by the French Admiral Nicolau Durand de Villegagnon in 1557 describing the invasion of Rio de Janeiro.

*Igreja Nossa Senhora do Carmo da Antiga Sé*

Cross the road and walk back to Rua 1 de Março to ★★ **Igreja Nossa Senhora do Carmo da Antiga Sé** ❷ (mass Monday 9am, Saturday 9am and 12.20pm; first and second Sunday of the month 9am), built in 1761 on the site of a previous church. With the arrival of the Portuguese royal family in 1808 the church was transformed into a royal chapel and cathedral, hosting the coronation of Pedro I in 1822, and remained Rio's cathedral until 1976. The font and *portada* were carved by Mestre Valentim.

Pass through the church, and on the left is a door with a passageway. On the right-hand wall of the passageway is a plaque stating that it is the last resting place of the remains of Pedro Álvares Cabral, the discoverer of Brazil, who was exhumed in 1903 and moved here from Santarem in Portugal by his family. The Convent of Nossa Senhora do Carmo was the residence of Queen D. Maria I and the convent was joined to the church building until 1857.

Between this church and the one next door is Beco dos Barbeiros, a small lane, usually closed, but at the far end – accessed from Rua do Carmo – is the last oratorio in the city: **Oratório de Nossa Senhora do Cabo da Boa Esperança (Boa Viagem)**. Rio used to have 70 of these statues for public prayer and to help illuminate the streets, all except this one have been removed. You can still see local people stop here to pray before going to work. The original statue, now priceless, can be seen in the sacristy in ★★ **Igreja Nossa Senhora da Ordem Terceira do Carmo** (Monday to Friday 8am–2pm, Saturday 8am–noon, mass Monday to Friday 9am, 10am, 11am, noon). Construction of the present church commenced in 1755 in the rococo and baroque styles, but there has been a chapel on the site since 1648. Built by slaves, using the dregs from the whaling industry as mortar, the church also had a tunnel

*Ingreja Nossa Senhora da Ordem Terceira do Carmo*

– now filled in – through which slaves could escape. The solid silver altar in the Capela-Mor dates from 1738, and probably came from the previous chapel. The Capela do Noviciado is a true masterpiece of Brazilian baroque, carved by Mestre Valentim in 1793.

*Confeitaria Colombo*

Turn right out of the church, and right again up Rua Sete de Setembro. Cross Avenida Rio Branco and you will find a small statue of a newspaper boy named after the famous newspaper *A Noite*, which used to be published here. Turn first right into Rua Gonçalves Dias and walk along to ★ **Confeitaria Colombo** ⑤③ (Monday to Friday 8.30am–7pm), a tea room/restaurant that typifies the *belle époque* of Rio de Janeiro. The decoration is Art Nouveau from 1913, with mirrors precariously imported from Belgium, marble from Italy, and carvings in jacaranda wood.

Continue along this street and turn left into Rua do Rosário. Straight ahead is Igreja de Nossa Senhora do Rosário e São Benedito, and to the left of the church down an alleyway, Rua Reitor Azevedo Amaral, and upstairs through a small door at the end, is the **Museu do Negro** ⑤④ (Monday to Friday 8am–4.30pm), dedicated to the history of the African in Brazil since the times of slavery. Note the bust of Anastácia, an Angolan princess, who grew up a free woman in Bahia, but because she said she wasn't a slave she was shackled and eventually died in Rio. She was buried in the church.

*Real Gabinete Português de Leiture*

Go to the back of the church and turn left towards Largo de São Francisco. Turn right in the square and walk along Rua Luís de Camões to the ★ **Real Gabinete Português de Leiture** ⑤⑤ (daily 9am–6pm). Created in 1837, this is one of the most valuable collections of Portuguese books outside Portugal. About 350,000 volumes, offered to Brazil as proof of recognition by Portugal, make up the collection.

*Fortune teller outside the Museu do Negro*

# Route 9

**Museu do Primeiro Reinado – Museu Nacional – Quinta da Boa Vista – Jardim Zoológico – Mangueira – Maracanã Stadium** *See map opposite*

Easily accessible from downtown, the Quinta da Boa Vista park was once a farm-garden owned by the royal family and later their residence. The park has excellent security, but tourists should remain alert while walking around its outskirts. (Buses 473, 472, 474, metro São Cristóvão and Metro Maracanã also serve this route.) The park is close to one of the city's most famous samba schools and the Maracanã Stadium.

*Museu do Primeiro Reinado*

**58**

**Museu do Primeiro Reinado ⑤⑥** (Avenida Pedro II, 293. Tuesday to Friday 11.30am–5pm, Saturday and Sunday 1–5pm) is also known as the House of the Marquesa de Santos. It depicts the history of Dom Pedro I and his affair with the Domitila de Castro Canto e Melo, with a collection of personal objects and letters. It was built in the neo-classic style with beautiful paintings and carvings on the walls by the French Artists' Mission. There is a concert on Tuesday and special tea once a month.

Connecting the museum and the park is the Corredor Imperial. The **Army Museum** is along this route as you walk in the direction of the entrance to **Quinta da Boa Vista ⑤⑦** (daily 8am–7pm). An important leisure parkland with trees, lakes, caves and gardens, it hasn't changed much since Imperial times and houses the National Museum and Rio's Zoological Garden.

*Quinta da Boa Vista*

**Museu Nacional** (Tuesday to Sunday 10am–4pm) is one of the largest natural history museums in South America with huge meteorites, pre-Columbian ceramics, dinosaur fossils and explanations about the peoples of Brazil with their different cultures. The Ancient Egyptian collection is the most extensive in South America and includes several mummies. The museum has more than four million pieces, some of which were owned by the royal family who lived here from 1809 until the Proclamation of the Republic in 1889.

*Parrot fashion, Jardim Zoológico*

Continue walking through the park in a westerly direction to the **Jardim Zoológico** (Zoological Garden) ⑤⑧ (Tuesday to Sunday 10am–4pm). Opened in 1945, it keeps around 2,500 different species, some extinct in the wild, including birds, mammals and reptiles from the Amazon, Pantanal and Atlantic Forest areas.

For those who are interested in Carnival and would like to know how the samba schools work, walk out of the park's west gate and turn right to **Mangueira**  (Sede Palácio do Samba, Rua Visconde de Niterói 1072), one of the most traditional samba schools in Rio since its foundation in 1928. Rehearsals are held mainly at weekends in the months leading up to the Carnival, but many other activities are held in this space.

Walk back about 150m (165yd) along Rua Visconde de Niterói, and cross the railway tracks towards Metro Maracanã station for the most famous stadium in Brazil, ★ **Maracanã Stadium and Sports Museum**  (Monday to Friday 9am–5pm, Saturday and Sunday 9am–3pm. Museum closed on game days. Match information, tel: 242 8806). The biggest football stadium in the world – it could hold 200,000 people until safety restrictions reduced its capacity by 14,000 – Maracanã was one of the most outstanding civil constructions in Brazil of the late-1940s. Needing 11,000 workers and 500,000 sacks of cement, it was built in only 665 days. Maracanã opened in time to host the 1950 World Cup soccer matches, including the final when Brazil was beaten 2-1 by Uruguay (one of the country's few defeats in the stadium – having played over 100 internationals here, it has lost just six). The stadium also saw Pelé score his 1,000th professional goal in 1969. It houses big religious events and musical shows as well, with performers such as Frank Sinatra, The Rolling Stones, Tina Turner, Prince, George Michael, Guns N' Roses, Sting and Madonna. In 1990 Paul McCartney attracted the largest paying audience ever to attend a solo artist's concert.

For a great soccer experience try to see a local match in Maracanã. Usually security is very good, and families are seated in grandstand seats. The largest, most popular Rio clubs are Flamengo, Botafogo, Vasco and Fluminense.

*Maracanã Stadium*

*Match in progress*

**59**

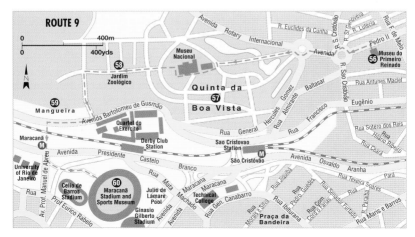

*Zone Oeste Beach*

# Route 10

### The Future of Rio

*'Try this one for size'*

**Barra Shopping – Autódromo Nelson Piquet – Rio Centro – Maciço de Gericinó/Serra da Mendanha – Parque Estadual Maciço da Pedra Branca – Zone Oeste Beaches – Casa do Pontal – Sítio Roberto Burle Marx** *See map opposite*

Rio is not just the famous Zona Sul with its busy streets and packed beaches. Much of the action in the past decade has moved west to an area known as Barra da Tijuca, which is seen as the future of Rio. It probably has more in common with modern-day Miami than historical Rio.

The area contains numerous modern shopping centers, including the biggest of them all, ★ **Barra Shopping** ❻❶ (Avenida das Américas, 4666 – Barra, tel: 325 3233), as well as the city's first multiplex cinemas; Rio's main theme park, **Terra Encantada** (Enchanted World, Avenida Ayrton Senna 421, Barra, tel: 421 4944; Wednesday to Sunday 10am–10pm); the motor racing circuit **Autódromo Nelson Piquet** (tel: 342 1313); the city's convention center, **Rio Centro** ❻❷, which hosted the Earth Summit in 1992; and one of Rio's main show venues, **Metropolitan** (tel: 421 1331), located in the Via Parque shopping center.

*Barra Shopping*

Barra is also home to the **Itanhangá Golf and Country Club** (Estrada da Barra, 2005 – Barra, tel: 494 2507); the six hole-par-3 Golden Green (Posto 7, Praia da Barra, tel: 433 3950), which is open to the public.

Strangely, and perhaps one reason why this area has been overlooked by most visitors, hotels of note are few and far between here.

The Barra area and beyond also offers plenty to those who prefer to get close to nature. Some of the most important areas of primeval forest are found here with rich vegetation, old farms and ecological parks. The predominant flora is *herbácea*, and the area also has rich fauna and birds that migrate here during the nesting season. The **Maciço do Gericinó/Serra da Mendanha** ⓺ (Monday to Friday 7am–5pm. Visits with authorisation only) is a reserve of *Mata Atlântica* forest that used to cover most of Brazil's coastline. Primeval trees grow up to 25m (82ft) high, and as late as 1979 two extinct volcanoes were discovered, one measuring 300m (1,000ft) in diameter. Ecological tours must be organized with specialist EMBRATUR registered guides (Rua Uruguaiana 174, Centro, tel: 509 6017 or Rua Professora Francisca Piragibe 80, Jacarepaguá, Taquara, tel: 445 3387).

*Parque Pedra Branca*

The **Parque Estadual Maciço da Pedra Branca** ⓺, which became a National Park in 1974, stretches northward from Praia dos Búzios in Barra de Guaratiba, and includes the hills of Jacarepaguá, Recreio dos Bandeirantes, Grumari, Barra de Guaratiba and Senador Camará. The park has various natural springs and the highest peak in Rio, Pico da Pedra Branca, at 1,250m (4,100ft).

**61**

**Zone Oeste Beaches**: **Praia da Barra** ⓺, 18km (11 miles) long, is not only the longest and most beautiful in the city but also one of the cleanest. **Recreio dos Bandeirantes** ⓺, a large rock at the end of Barra Beach, is known because of its green waters and generous arch of sand called **Praia do Pontal**. As the beach is at the end of a number of popular bus routes, this area can get very busy at the weekends. **Prainha** has only 150m (165yd) of white sand in a protected area, and is a surfers' paradise. **Grumari** ⓺ has a very beautiful beach, accessed by the

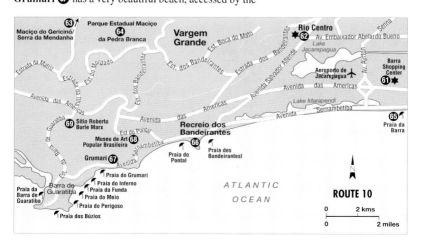

Grumari road, with reddish sand, strong waves, rocks, two small islands and a couple of bar-restaurants. In the week it will be relatively deserted as it is difficult to reach without a car. The film *Blame It On Rio*, starring Michael Caine, was shot here. **Praias dos Búzios, do Perigoso, do Meio, da Funda** and **do Inferno** retain their primitive natural charm because they can be reached only by foot along mountain trails through the forest. **Barra de Guaratiba**, a fishing colony still keeps the tranquil atmosphere of the past. They are included in Parque Nacional the Pedra Branca, which is a model biological reserve where all construction is banned.

*Culture encapsulated at Casa do Pontal*

**Museu de Arte Popular Brasileira – Casa do Pontal** ⑱ (Estrada do Pontal 3295, Recreio dos Bandeirantes, between Prainha and Vargem Grande, tel: 490 3278 for groups; Tuesday to Sunday 9am–5pm). This is about one hour from Barra Shopping on bus No. 702 or 703 from Terminal Joatinga. With a collection of 5,000 pieces, it is the largest museum of Brazilian folk art, reflecting its culture, folklore, religion and music, and was founded by the French designer Jacques Van de Beuque, who has been building the collection for over half a century.

According to the International Council of Museums (ICOM), associated with UNESCO, 'It may be considered a true anthropological museum, the only one in Brazil to afford a comprehensive view of the life and culture of the Brazilian people.' The museum has an interesting book shop and café.

*Veranda at Sítio Roberto Burle Marx*

Around the corner at Estrada da Barra de Guaratiba 2019, **Sítio Roberto Burle Marx** ⑲ (guided tours at 9.30am and 1.30pm must be scheduled in advance, tel: 410 1412 or 410 1171 9am–4pm). Take bus No. 387 (Marambaia–Passeio), or the executive bus (Santa Cruz) via Barra or Campo Grande via Barra, get off at the Ipiranga gas station and ask directions. Burle Marx (1909–94) was an architect, landscape designer and artist. The Copacabana street pavement design and Flamengo Park are some of his works. He started to collect plants at the age of six and when he was 40, in 1949, he bought this land with his brother Siegfried who helped him to administrate it and collect the plants. The site has more than 3,500 species of plants, a botanical library and his art studios with his paintings in them. Marx also collected paintings and sculptures by national and internationally renowned artists, which are displayed in the main house. In 1985 he donated the entire site to the Brazilian Government as a trust. Marx's famous chef, Sr. César, the only person allowed to cook for him, and who accompanied him everywhere, now runs his own seafood restaurant almost opposite the front gate.

# Further Sights

The following sights are all within walking distance of Metro Botafogo (*see map on pages 18–19*):

**Casa Rui Barbosa** (Rua São Clemente 134, Botafogo. Tuesday to Friday 9am–4.15pm, Saturday to Sunday 2–5.15pm; free on Sunday). Born in 1849, Rui Barbosa became a solicitor, journalist, politician and diplomat. His house, which has been kept in its original state since his death, is a fascinating time capsule telling the story of this great man who wrote the Constitution in 1890 and defended human rights.

**Museu do Índio** (Rua das Palmeiras 55, Botafogo. Tuesday to Friday 10am–5.30pm, Saturday to Sunday 1–5pm). This museum gives an insight into the lives of 220 different Indian tribes, with huts, musical instruments, weapons and dress. There is a shop selling some superb Indian artefacts.

*Ceramics at Museu do Indio*

**Museu Villa-Lobos** (Rua Sorocaba 200, Botafogo. Monday to Friday 10am–5.30pm). Heitor Villa-Lobos (1887–1959) was considered the greatest composer in the Americas during his lifetime. This exhibition in his house shows his personal objects and musical instruments.

Other places within the city that are easily accessible by metro or bus include:

**Museu Carmen Miranda** (Avenida Rui Barbosa, opposite No. 560, in the center of the park. Nearest metro: Flamengo. Tuesday to Saturday 11am–5pm). Unfortunately housed in what looks like a bomb shelter, this is essential viewing for Carmen Miranda fans, with film stills and videos of the famous singer and actress, as well as a large collection of her clothes and shoes.

*Carmen Miranda and her shoes*

**Museu da Cidade** (Estrada Santa Marinha, Parque da Cidade, Gávea. Tuesday to Sunday 11am–5pm) is in the middle of a pretty park with a small chapel, but tourists are advised to arrive by taxi. The museum is in a large 19th-century colonial house and has a photographic collection of old Rio showing scenes of well-known streets, as well as models depicting the original coastline around the city.

**Museu da Vida** (FIOCRUZ) (Fundacão Oswaldo Cruz, Avenida Manguinhos, tel: 590 6747. Buses 372, 373, 374, 395 from downtown. Monday to Friday 8am–5pm). The Museum of Life is an interactive science center housed on the Oswaldo Cruz Foundation campus on Avenida Brasil on the way out to the airport. Along with the permanent health institute collection, the museum is divided into several interesting areas, including a Disney-style train ride aboard the Science Train, ecological trails, the Biological Experimental Center, Science On-stage area and many more science-as-entertainment exhibits. It is considered a center of excellence for international research, and is the largest vaccine center in South America.

**Niterói**, just across the bay from Rio, reveals some interesting treasures for those prepared to look. Reached by bus from Rio, by car, or more easily by ferry from Praça XV (*see map on pages 40–41*). The road (buses 119, 154, 413, 415, 455, 474) from Rio passes over the Rio-Niterói Bridge. Opened in 1974, it is 18km (11 miles) long and 60m (196ft) high in the center, and was considered the most important civil engineering feat in Brazil at the time.

*Museu do Inga*

In the center of Niterói visit the ★ **Museu do Ingá** (Rua Presidente Pedreira 78. Monday to Friday 11am–5pm, Saturday to Sunday 1–5pm) with its collection of 4,800 pieces, including furniture, paintings and porcelain, plus a fine selection of engravings, some of which are produced in the workshops run in the museum's own studios; ★ **Catedral de Niterói** (Praça Dom Pedro II. Daily 9am–6pm); **Teatro Municipal João Caetano** (Rua XV de Novembro 35, tel: 717 1551 for details of guided tours and programme listings), built in 1824 and one of the most important theaters in Brazil; and **Igreja Nossa Senhora da Conceição** (Rua da Conceição 216. Tuesday to Saturday 7–11am and 2–6pm, Saturday and Sunday 7–11am), a lovely little church dating from 1663.

*Igreja Nossa Senhora da Conceição*

Three places that are close to Niterói and worth a visit by bus or taxi are:

★ **Museu Antonio Parreiras** (Rua Tiradentes 47, Ingá. Tuesday to Friday 11am–5pm, Saturday to Sunday 3–6pm). The museum houses an exhibition of mainly seascapes and forest scenes around Rio de Janeiro by Antonio Parreiras (1860–1937).

★★ **Museu de Arte Contemporânea** (Mirante da Boa Viagem. Tuesday to Sunday 11am–6pm, *see picture on page 75*). Designed by the architect Oscar Niemeyer, this was opened in 1991 to house contemporary art exhibitions. The champagne glass-shaped building gives a superb 360-degree vista which includes a spectacular view back towards Rio.

★★ **Fortaleza de Santa Cruz** (Estrada General Eurico Gaspar Dutra. Daily 9am–5pm in summer, 9am–4pm in winter). Access to the fort is only by car or taxi, or by a bus operated by the Viação Miramar Bus Company. Bus No. 33, from Terminal João Gulart in the center, leaves at 11am, 11.30am, noon and 12.30pm, and passes inside the fort road; then visitors can return on the 4pm, 4.30pm, 5pm or 5.30pm bus. Constructed in 1555 by the French, the fort commanded a strategic position at the mouth of Guanabara Bay. In 1567 Mem de Sá expelled the French, and the fort was enlarged.

# Excursion 1

*Transport in Petrópolis*

Petrópolis – The Imperial City *See map on pages 66–7*

Visitors don't automatically associate tropical Rio with cooling mountain resorts, but they should. Since the time of the royal family, residents of Rio have been coming to the mountains and towns of Petrópolis and Teresópolis to escape the summer heat. Today, they are as popular as ever, especially at the weekend.

*Mirante do Cristo en route to Petrópolis*

**Petrópolis 'Cidade Imperial'** (1½ hours' journey from Rodoviária Novo Rio. Company: Fácil e única; from 5.15am then about every 20 minutes until midnight. Petrotur, the city's tourist board, has a special telephone number with information in English: in Petrópolis tel: 1516, from outside Petrópolis tel: 0800 241 1516) is only 67km (41 miles) from Rio, at an altitude of 809m (2,654ft), in the Serra da Estrela Mountains. The 'Imperial City' of Petrópolis was given this title because of its popularity with the royal family who would stay here during summer, allowing much of the diplomatic corps to follow them.

Dom Pedro I 'discovered' this region in 1822, and bought a farm here. Later Dom Pedro II built a summer residence, which in 1943 became the present ★ **Museu Imperial** (Rua da Imperatriz 220. Tuesday to Saturday 11am–5.30pm; Sunday 11am–4.45pm). It contains 12,000 pieces of national culture and other important objects from the time of the monarchs.

★ **Casa de Santos Dumont** (Rua do Encanto 22. Tuesday to Sunday 9.30am–5.30pm) was the summer residence of the aviation pioneer (*see page 43*). The architecture reflects the life of the eccentric inventor.

*Casa de Santos Dumont*

★★ **Palácio de Cristal** (Rua Alfredo Pachá; Tuesday to Sunday 9am–5pm). Built for Princesa Isabel, the prefabricated building is made from French cast iron and glass, and was erected for agricultural and horticultural shows. Today it is used for exhibitions.

*Catedral São Pedro de Alcântara*

**Catedral São Pedro de Alcântara** (Rua São Pedro de Alcântara 60. Tuesday to Sunday 8am–noon and 2–6pm). Constructed in French 18th-century Gothic style, its foundation stone was laid in 1884. The interior houses the Imperial Chapel where the remains of Dom Pedro II, Dona Teresa Cristina, Conde D'Eu and Princesa Isabel are laid to rest.

**Casa do Barão de Mauá** (Praça da Canfluência 03. Monday to Friday 8.30am–6pm). Constructed in the neo-classical style, the house has a unique window arrangement to allow ventilation. Ask the tourist board, whose offices are in the building, for a demonstration.

★ **Rio Negro – Palácio dos Presidentes** (Avenida Koeler 255. Wednesday to Sunday 9.30am–5pm). Since 1903 this has been the official summer holiday residence of the presidents of Brazil and when in use is closed to the public. The floors have beautiful parquetry designs and some of the furniture won a prize in the 1889 Paris Furniture Exhibition.

*Casa de Petrópolis*

**Casa da Princesa** (Avenida Koeler 42. Tuesday to Sunday 10am–6pm). Built in 1857 and sold to Princesa Isabel and Conde D'Eu in 1877, the house soon became a landmark. The pen Isabel used to sign the decree giving slaves their freedom has only recently been put on exhibition.

**Casa de Petrópolis** (Avenida Ipiranga 716. Tuesday to Sunday 11am–7pm). This is known locally as the house of seven mistakes, and visitors try to spot the differences in design from one half of the house to the other. Built in 1884, it still has much of its original furniture and fittings, and now hosts art exhibitions and shows.

# Excursion 2

## Búzios – Rio's Playground

**Búzios** (Ônibus from Rodoviária Novo Rio: three hours' journey with bus company 1001. About every two hours from 6.30am until 7.15pm and at 8.15pm on Friday).

Búzios is a town on a peninsular 180km (111 miles) up the coast from Rio with some of Brazil's greatest beaches. It also has some very good inns and restaurants offering excellent value for money. It is where many of the Cariocas spend their weekends and holiday celebrations, including Carnival and the New Year. While it is possible to visit Búzios in a day, it is better to spend one or more nights in and around the village.

*Schooner diving*

In the 17th century this remote peninsular was invaded by the English and French, used by pirates as a base, and as a port for illegal trafficking of wood and slaves. Today locals believe the ghosts of the old slaves and pirates still inhabit the streets at night.

Búzios remained a sleepy fishing village until 1964 when Brigitte Bardot was discovered here by the paparazzi and exposed the town to international publicity. Since then it has been a popular haunt for 'beautiful people' from around the world.

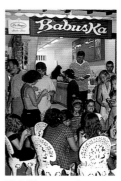

**67**

The old street of ★★★ **Rua das Pedras**, which gets its name from the giant uneven paving stones, and has sophisticated boutiques, bars and restaurants offerings all sorts of specialty dishes, is the center of the town's famous nightlife. It is legendary that the local population doesn't get up until after lunch, and in fact many of the eateries don't even bother to open for lunch.

*Nightlife on Rua das Pedras*

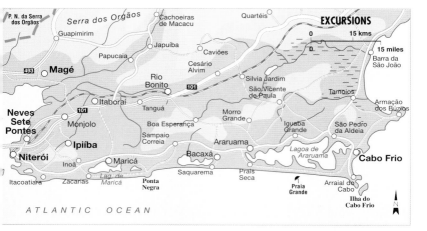

*Praia Brava*

*Praia Azeda*

*Lunch on the Escuna Buziana*

Fortunately this does not apply to the excellent restaurants in the back streets.

★★★ **All the beaches** on the peninsular are superb and have their own character. Nearest to the center are **do Canto**, **da Armação**, **dos Ossos** and **Azeda**. Further round the point of the peninsular is **Praia João Fernandes**, and on the other side are the more secluded beaches of **Forno** and **Brava**. **Praia Olho de Boi**, one of the few nudist beaches in Brazil, is reached in about 20 minutes by a mountainous trail from Praia Brava. The beach with the warmest water is **Praia da Tartaruga**, so named because sea turtles are attracted by the warm waters to lay their eggs here.

The daytime activities center around the beaches or water sports. Ponto-Mar (Rua das Pedras 212; tel: 024 6232173) organizes diving courses. It is also possible to hire diving equipment and a boat on a daily basis.

The ★★ **Escuna Buziana** (tel: 024-623 6760; main jetty 9.30am, 10.30am, 12.30am, 1.30pm, 3.30pm and 4.30pm) is a schooner that makes regular trips to the main beaches. This is a good way to get to know the area and the crew makes sure everyone has a good time with special safety attention paid to children and non-swimmers when the boat stops at the different beach locations.

Most of the accommodations in Búzios are in *pousadas* (small inns) with lots of character but a limited number of rooms. Don't expect major resort hotels, so ask a travel agent to get you a room if you are going for the weekend; or you can simply turn up and take pot luck if you are going during the week.

Búzios has a very well-organized tourism association (tel: 0800 24 99 99), which can offer advice and practical help. Also well worth checking are the Búzios websites at www.buziosonline.com.br.

# Excursion 3

## The Islands and Parati *See map on pages 66–7*

Spreading 280km (175 miles) west of Rio towards São Paulo is a region known as the ★★ **Costa Verde** (Green Coast). It contains some of the world's most beautiful and spectacular coastline, including Angra dos Reis (King's Cove) with an estimated 365 tropical islands. The easiest way to visit them from Rio is on an organized tour aboard a traditional Brazilian schooner (*saveiro*). The boats, which sail from the village of Itacuruçá (about 1½ hours' drive from Rio), normally visit four or five islands during the day, giving plenty of opportunity for swimming in the sheltered waters of Sepetiba Bay. The trips can be booked in most hotels and travel agents in Rio.

*The harbor at Angra*

The scenery along the coast road really gets dramatic beyond Itacuruçá, so another option is to continue to the town of **Angra dos Reis**. Sr. Sergio Ricardo of Maravilha (tel: 365 4997) operates a boat service to explore the islands and also offers diving and fishing packages. Notable among the islands are: **Ilhas das Botinas**, two tiny islands that are excellent for snorkeling; and **Ilha Grande**, the biggest island in the bay, which has great beaches, small villages with hotels, bars, restaurants but no cars.

*Snorkeling at*
*Ilhas das Botinas*            **69**

Hotel do Bosque (tel: 024 363 3130 or 021 521 8297), a private ecological reserve by the River Mambucaba, offers horse-riding and jeep and boat tours at what is considered one of the best locations in the bay. Guided tours of the local ecological trails can be arranged by Jose Antonio Martins Rosa (tel: 024 365 4330).

Another worthwhile excursion is to continue beyond Angra to the historic village of ★★ **Parati**, located 250km (155 miles) west of Rio. As the drive is over three hours, it is worth staying overnight and the town has over 80 colonial inns. Parati has been inhabited since 1650 and at one time rivalled Rio as a port for shipping the gold from Minas Gerais to Portugal. It lost its strategic importance in the 19th century with the opening of a new road between Rio and São Paulo, with the result that a large part of the town was left untouched. UNESCO considers Parati to be one of the most important surviving examples of colonial architecture. The streets are paved with irregular stones that form a canal to drain off storm water and allow the sea to enter and wash them at full moon and high tides.

*Paving at Parati*

Visitors looking for quality beach time may consider the Club Med village of Rio das Pedras, an all-inclusive resort located in its own bay just over halfway from Rio to Parati. One of the world's most exclusive eating places is the tiny island restaurant of **Ilha da Mandala** (*see page 81*), accessible only by boat (*see above* for services).

# Music

Brazil has some of the most sophisticated rhythms in the world, musical styles such as the *bossa nova* which took the world by its ear and its heart with songs like *The Girl from Ipanema* in the early 1960s. That decade, arguably the best for Brazilian music, was full of optimism. Juscelino Kubitschek had organized the building of Brasília, and film, theater, dance and painting all thrived.

Brazil's musical history started with African influences brought by the slaves, and schools of music already existed in Bahia in the early 17th century. The arrival of the royal family had a major impact, with music being composed and played especially for the Royal Court. At the end of the 19th century, Carlos Gomes (1836–96) was sent to Italy by Dom Pedro II to study music and was influenced by Verdi and Ponchielli. His best-known work is the opera *O Guarani*, based on an Indian romance by the Brazilian writer Jose de Alencar.

*Carlos Gomes*

In the 19th century *choro*, a Brazilian brand of popular urban music, developed using flute, ukulele, clarinet, viola, cavaquinho, trombone and some percussion instruments. Its success was helped by improvements in instrumental virtuosity and also by the melancholic inflection that justifies the name *choro* (literally 'crier'). *Chorinho* ('little crier') is a light variant in which the melancholic line tends to be expressed through the instrument. *Choro* was born through the groups called *seresteiros*, who played the sad yet uplifting music in the city's nightclubs; Pixinguinha (1889–1973) was an important member of one of these. The first *choros* were written around 1870 by the composer and flautist Joaquim Antonio da Silva Callado (1848–80) and the conductor and composer Chiquinha Gonzaga (1847–1935). He was an exponent of erudite popular music, while she was the first woman to play in public and a pioneer when playing *chorinho* on the piano. In 1899 she composed one of the first Carnival songs, *Abre Alas*.

*Seresteiros musician figures in Casa do Pontal*

The composer Ernesto Nazare (1847–1934) was strongly influenced by typical popular Brazilian music and ballroom music imported from Europe. Heitor Villa-Lobos (1887–1959) brought the modernity of avant-garde techniques from Europe and introduced folklore, melodies and rhythms to symphonic compositions. He created the first really expressive Brazilian music, writing 14 famous *choros*, the *Bachianas Brasileiras*, which are still as fresh as ever today.

## Fighting style

Another early Brazilian genre of music and dance is *capoeira*, a ritualized form of combat dance evolved from a fighting style that originated in Angola and arrived with

*Gal Costa sings*

the Bantu slaves. In colonial times when the slaves were caught practicing this marshal art they were punished, so it developed into a barefoot dance with music and song to cover up the actual fighting. Over the years *capoeira* has become a highly athletic sport and a respected art form which is now popular all over Brazil, and can be seen demonstrated on the beach in Rio and in the town squares. The musical backing includes the *berimbau*, a bow-shaped piece of wood with one metal string and a gourd-shaped resonator. The player shakes the bow and strikes the taut wire with a rod, which sets the beat for the dancers to follow. *Capoeira* has crossed over into more mainstream Brazilian culture and influenced songs like Baden Powell and Vinícius de Moraes' *Berimbau* and Gilberto Gil's *Domingo no Parque*.

### Samba and Carnival

Thanks largely to Carnival, samba, after *bossa nova*, is probably the best-known musical form to come out of Brazil. Samba's origins date back to the early part of the 20th century and helped transform popular Brazilian music. Samba, as presented at Carnival by the samba schools, the *samba-enredo* (story samba), is quite different from the *samba-cancao* (samba song) which first came to popular attention in the 1930s. The latter emphasizes the melody and more sophisticated lyrics, while the former is more rhythmic and designed around the school's selected theme.

*Samba schools parade in the Sambódromo*

In the beginning samba and *choro* were performed by groups that played a kind of music that was considered radical. The main composers – Sinho (1888–1930), Canhoto (1889–1928), Pixinguinha, Donga (1889–1974), and Cartola (1908–1980) – had connections with the *morros* (hillside slum areas). Donga and Mauro de Almeida composed the first samba to be recorded, *Pelo Telefone*, in 1917, while in 1929 Cartola and his fellow composer, Carlos Cachaca, founded the samba schools. Their second one, Estacao Primeira de Mangueira, became an integral part of the fabric that is Rio's Carnival over the years, and it was Carnival that helped to fuel the demand for new sambas to sing and parade.

Samba schools are not schools in the traditional sense, but clubs that draw predominantly poor communities together for music and dance. For Carnival each will select its theme and around this the school's top composers will write, one song being chosen for the parade. The equivalent of a film or theatrical director will then take over and, helped by artists, designers and choreographers, will turn that song into an extravaganza mixing song and dance with the visual splendor that is Carnival. Each school's samba is a unique artistic presentation.

## Bossa nova explodes

*Bossa nova* arrived in the late 1950s, and by the early 1960s Brazilian music was suddenly known throughout the world. *Bossa nova* had an intimate style which exulted the simplicity of things in life with romantic lyrics, many about the city of Rio. Copacabana and Ipanema were the cradle of the most important musical movement that Brazil had ever seen. It was launched in 1958 with the album *Cancao do Amor Demais*, sung by Elizeth Cardoso and featuring the compositions of Vinícius de Moraes and Tom Jobim and guitar of João Gilberto. Gilberto's own album, *Chega de Saudade*, arranged by Jobim and released the following year, helped bring *bossa nova* national acclaim.

International recognition was not long in coming. American saxophonist Stan Getz was one of the first to make the breakthrough with the album *Jazz Samba* in 1962. It included both *Desafinado* and *Samba de Uma Nota So* and went to number one in the US charts. A legendary concert at Carnegie Hall in New York followed, which united Brazilian musicians with their North American counterparts. Two years and three albums later, Getz joined Jobim and Gilberto to record *Getz/Gilberto*, an album that featured, almost as an afterthought, Gilberto in a duet with his wife, Astrud. *The Girl From Ipanema*, the lyrical story of the lifestyle of the Carioca, was an international hit and brought fame to the lyricist/poet Vinicius and its composer, Jobim. The bar where they composed many of their hits is still going in Ipanema (*see page 30*).

Jobim's body of work has become one of the most recorded in the history of popular music and at one time rivalled even the Beatles. 'But,' as he once noted, 'there were four of them!' Tragically, Jobim died in 1994 of complications following what should have been a relatively straightforward operation in New York. At the time, he was as prolific and popular as ever.

*The late great Antonio Carlos 'Tom' Jobim*

**73**

*Stan Getz*

*Mosterio de Sao Bento*

*Sacristy painting of St Anthony in the Igreja de Santo Antônio*

*'Café' by Cândido Portinari*

# Art and Architecture

## Visual arts

In Rio the history of art can be divided into three phases: colonial, academic and modern. In colonial times, the baroque period, artists had a prosperous relationship with the Catholic church, with major commissions to decorate the interiors of the churches. These were carved and covered with gold, and had painted panels on the walls. Painting, sculpture and carving at that time all showed images of Jesus Christ and the different saints. The origin of the styles was Portuguese, brought to Brazil by a respected artist, Mestre Francisco Xavier de Brito. With time, however, this style was modified by the influence of new artists who had different ideas and cultural backgrounds. These new artists were often children of a slave and a Portuguese, as was the case with the most important sculptor and woodcarver, Mestre Valentim da Fonseca e Silva (1745–1813), who was responsible for many of the famous sculptures and fountains in Rio.

When Dom João VI, the Portuguese monarch, arrived, he encouraged intellectual activity in Rio with the founding of cultural institutions such as the Royal Press and the National Library. The French Artists' Mission followed in 1816 with the painters Jean-Baptiste Debret and Nicholas Taunay and the architect Auguste Grandjean de Montigny. They had come to Rio at the invitation of Dom João VI to help style the 'modernization' plan for the city as a royal capital. They taught in the Academia de Belas Artes, which later became the National Museum of Fine Arts in Cinelândia, and their neoclassical influence remained strong until around 1900, when Brazilian artists began to be influenced by French Impressionists.

Works by modern artists such as Cândido Portinari and Emiliano Di Cavalcanti are on show in Rio's Museum of Modern Art in Flamengo Park, a building designed by another famous artist, sculptor and landscape designer, Robert Burle Marx (1909–94). The modernists wished to shock the academic establishment, and the 1922 movement, in which Brazilian artists expressed their dissatisfactions with 'academic' art at São Paulo's Week of Modern Art, coincided with changes in outlook about the country generally. It became the catalyst for a search for new values and a rejection of the old European artistic stereotypes. Emiliano Di Cavalcanti (1897–1976), a founder of Brazil's 1922 movement, was a true bohemian from a family of poets. He liked to frequent Rio's underworld and paint seductive *mulata* (ex-slave) women.

Brazil is also one of the main countries to produce naïve art, and has the largest collection of paintings in this style at the Museu International de Arte Naïf (*see page 23*).

## Architecture

Secular buildings in the colonial time bore the marks of simplicity, while religious buildings, by different Catholic Orders, were constructed with great beauty from good materials that have lasted until today. The baroque style, adopted in the 17th and 18th centuries, featured interiors rich in detail and ornamentation, in contrast with the modest exterior. The neo-classical style arrived with the French Mission, and this was of great importance for the progression of art generally in Brazil.

At the beginning of the 20th century the eclectic style was inspired by historical styles and the influence of Art Nouveau with nature as its main theme. From 1902, Rio underwent a great urban transformation under Pereira Passos. The most profound change was the opening of Avenida Central, now Avenida Rio Branco, at 33m (108ft) wide and 1.8km (1 mile) long; about 650 houses and many *cortiços* (slum tenements) were demolished to make way for it. To replace these colonial buildings new ones were built in the *eclético* style. The best examples are the Municipal Theater, inspired by the Paris Opera and planned by Francisco de Oliveira Passos, the National Library and the National Museum of Fine Arts in the Cinelândia area.

The neo-colonial movement tried to promote a national style around 1910 with a major architectural research project, but it lost direction when people realized that all the styles in Brazil had, at that time, been imported from Europe. However, the neo-classical idea for a national style was adopted officially and architectural competitions were organized. Such a competition, to find a design for Brazil's pavilion at the 1925 Philadelphia Exposition, was won by Lúcio Costa who in 1930 was invited to be Director of the Escola National de Belas Artes. He made radical changes in the teaching methods inviting Le Corbusier, the Swiss-French modern architect, to lecture to students.

After the 1925 International Exhibition of Arts in Paris, new European styles influenced Rio, and in the 1930s and 1940s Art Deco appeared. During the administration of President Getúlio Vargas, who encouraged industrialization and civic construction, many residential buildings were built with five floors in the 1930s, rising to 12 or more in the 1940s. The Zona Sul started to grow vertically, while the poor areas and *favelas* expanded horizontally or on to the hillsides. Copacabana is a good example of this.

Gradually Brazilian architects have gained their own identity, and some examples of modern architecture are the Santos Dumont Airport by the Roberto Brothers; Museum of Modern Art by Affonso Eduardo Reidy; Architecture and Urbanism University by Jorge Machado Moreira; and Museum of Contemporary Art in Niterói, the work of Brazil's most famous architect, Oscar Niemeyer.

*Art Nouveau residence*

*Art Deco entrance*

*Niemeyer's Museum of Contemporary Art*

# Food and Drink

Rio is full of restaurants and, with few exceptions, every international taste is catered for and the quality generally good. Even accounting for Rio's large middle-class population, most of the better places to eat are not expensive by European standards and there are thousands of small family-run restaurants and bars that serve food at very accessible prices. From Japanese to Chinese, from Italian to French, it seems you can find a good restaurant around every corner. Rio also has its share of burger bars and American fast-food establishments.

As far as traditional Brazilian fare is concerned, *coxinha* is chicken in a savory dough ball, and *pastel* is a filo pastry case with a sweet or savory filling of meat, fish or vegetables that is fried while you wait. These are meals in themselves and can be bought on almost every street corner along with *churros*, a deep-fried dough stick filled with condensed milk or jam, which make a great dessert.

Originally from Minas Gerais, a state famous for its cheese, *pão de queijo* is cheese bread which is eaten at any time of the day but especially for breakfast with strong espresso coffee. A small cup of coffee is called a *cafezinho* and is usually laced with sugar and without milk. You will normally be offered a free *cafezinho* after a meal (and at any time of day in better stores and large supermarkets).

The national dish is *feijoada*, a bubbling cauldron of meat and black beans. Originally eaten by slaves, it used parts of the pig that were left over by the slave owners, such as the feet, ears, nose and tail. Nowadays it is the national dish eaten all over Brazil, especially at lunchtime on Saturday, and has been refined with varieties of dried, salted and smoked meats accompanied by rice, spring greens and *farofa*, a side dish made from manioc flour. *Feijoada* is usually served with *caipirinha*, a strong alcoholic apéritif made from *cachaça* (Brazil's strong liquor distilled from sugar cane), lemon juice, crushed lemon, ice and sugar. Cariocas spend a long time over their *feijoada*, and the Saturday lunch has become an institution, spreading well into the late afternoon or early evening.

The *churrascaria*, or barbecue, is another strong Rio institution. Restaurants specializing in this, also known as *churrascarias*, serve a buffet of vegetables, salads and so on, and waiters bring huge freshly barbecued cuts of meat and fish to your table (*rodízio* service). If you like meat, you will love the *churrascarias* because the beef from the southern states of Brazil is among the tastiest in the world. They also serve chicken, lamb, pork and fish, and keep serving until you indicate you have eaten enough.

Rice and beans are the everyday accompaniments for beef, chicken or fish dishes, along with salad. Meals are

*Opposite: try Brazil's national dish of feijoada*

*Al fresco treats at the Caesar Park Hotel*

**77**

*Buffet in a churrascaria restaurant*

*Barbecued palmito (palm cabbage)*

*A Santa Teresa favorite*

usually served with *cerveja* (beer), which is best drunk ice cold. *Chopp* is draught beer, and Cariocas drink it in cafés and bars at any time, usually accompanied by snacks like *peixe frito* (fried fish) and *batata frita* (potatoes).

Rio's restaurants generally stock a very drinkable selection of wines from Brazil and its South American neighbors, most notably Argentina and Chile. Of the soft drinks, *guaraná* comes from the *guaraná* fruit, which grows in the Amazon. In its natural state it has medicinal properties including being a stimulant, but commercially bottled *guaraná* is considered an alternative to cola.

As Brazilians tend to eat late, most restaurants serve until midnight or later. Those in the city center, the business heart of Rio, mainly close during the weekend.

### Restaurant selection
The following suggestions from Rio's restaurants are listed according to four categories: $$$$=very expensive; $$$=expensive; $$=moderate; $=inexpensive.

**78**

*Botafogo*
**Clube Gourmet**, Rua General Polidoro 186, tel: 295 3494. Relaxed and stylish with some of Rio's most interesting, innovative dishes. A small, ever-changing menu. $$$
**Sol e Mar**, Avenida Repórter Nestor Moreira 11, tel: 543 1663. Excellent seafood and fish beautifully presented with a romantic view of Sugar Loaf. Dancing. $$$

*Centro*
**Alba Mar**, Praça Marechal Ancora 184, tel: 240 8378. Fish by the dock in an old circular market building. $$$

*Confeitaria Colombo*

**Confeitaria Colombo**, Rua Gonçalves Dias 32, tel: 232 2300. Excellent for afternoon tea or a full lunch. $$$
**Arco Imperial**, Travessa do Comércio 13, tel: 508 9190. Good 'buffet per kilo' with barbecue (*see page 55*). $$
**Grill 22**, Rua 1 de Março 22, tel: 509 2290. Grill/buffet. $$.
**Restaurante Panorâmico 42**, Rua da Assembléia 10/4201 (same building as Riotur), tel: 531 2920. Good buffet and fantastic views from the 42nd floor. $

*Al fresco on Avenida Atlântica*

*Copacabana and Leme*
**Asian Corner**, Avenida Atlântica 3264 (in the Rio Othon Palace), tel: 522 1522. Excellent Asian cuisine and a breathtaking beach view. Try the Estância or Skylab restaurants in the same hotel for international food. Formal. $$$$
**Cipriani**, Avenida Atlântica 1702, tel: 548 7070. Within the Copacabana Palace. Many Italian dishes were developed in the Venice hotel of the same name. Formal $$$$
**Le Saint Honoré**, Avenida Atlântica 1020, tel: 247 9506. Outstanding French restaurant located on top of the Méridien Hotel. Memorable views and dishes. $$$$

**Deck**, Avenida Atlântica 2316A, tel: 547 3535. Seafood and fish next to the beach. $$$

*Romantic setting and fine seafood at Sol e Mar*

**Mariu's**, Avenida Atlântica 290, tel: 542 2393. One of the best and most popular *churrascaria rodízios* in Rio. $$$

**Restaurante a Marisqueira**, Rua Barata Ribeiro 232, tel: 547 3920. Renowned for its cuisine. $$$

**Casa do Barão**, Rua Barão de Ipanema 76, tel: 257 3340. Modern '*comida por kilo*' (buffet by kilo) restaurant with a fresh selection of food. $$

**Grill Inn**, Rua Barata Ribeiro 638, tel: 256 1194. Buffet of salads with barbecue and pastas. $$

**Kicê Sucos**, Avenida Nossa Senhora de Copacabana 1033, tel: 287 2141. Juice bar with *açaí* (tropical) fruit juice. $

**Mala e Cuia**, Raimundo Corrêa ST 34, tel: 235 7994. Excellent food from Minas Gerais with buffet and à la carte and rural décor. $$

**Aipo & Aipim**, Avenida Nossa Senhora de Copacabana 391, tel: 255 6285. Informal family-run buffet. $

**Cirandinha**, Avenida Nossa Senhora de Copacabana 719. Air-conditioned tea room with pizzas and ices. $

**Monchique Churrascaria Rodízio**, Avenida Nossa Senhora de Copacabana 796-A, tel: 255 8840. A family-run barbecue. $

*Flamengo*

**Alcaparra**, Praia do Flamengo 150, tel: 558 3937. Brazilian and international food. Romantic atmosphere with dark wood paneling. $$$

**Casa da Suiça**, Rua Candido Mendes 15, tel: 252 5182. Traditional and popular with the business community for lunch and with everyone else for dinner. Consistently good with a Swiss theme. $$$

**Majórica**, Rua Senador Vergueiro 11, tel: 285 6789. One of the city's most traditional barbecue houses and still one of the best. Not a *rodízio* – you choose what you want. $$$

*Casa da Feijoada*

*Lord Jim Pub*

*Ipanema*

**Petronius**, Avenida Vieira Souto 460 (in the Caesar Park Hotel, tel: 525 2525). Delicious seafood and a spectacular view of the beach. $$$$

**L'Arlecchino**, Rua Prudente de Morais 1387, tel: 259 7745. For nearly a decade the most consistent, adventurous Italian restaurant in Rio. Excellent wine cellar. $$$

**Casa da Feijoada**, Rua Prudente de Morais 10, tel: 523 4994. Traditional pork and beans stew. $$$

**Esplanada Grill**, Rua Barão de Torre 600, tel: 239 6028. Best and smartest grill house in Rio. $$$

**Lord Jim Pub**, Rua Paul Redfern 63, tel: 259 3047. English pub food. $$$

**Porção**, Rua Barão da Torre 218, tel: 521 0999. The best *churrascaria rodízio* in Ipanema. An institution. $$$

**Satyricon**, Rua Barão da Torre 192, tel: 521 0627. Stylish restaurant with excellent seafood and Italian dishes. $$$

**Fazendola**, Rua Jangadeiros 14, tel: 523 8641. Very tasty '*comida por kilo*' restaurant. $$.

**Garota de Ipanema**, Rua Vinícius de Moraes 49, tel: 523 3787. Brazilian food steeped in the history of the famous song. $$

*Jardim Botânico*

**Troisgros**, Rua Custódio Serrão 62, tel: 537 8582. One of Rio's finest restaurants. Chef Claude Troisgros, son of the famous Pierre Troisgros, is a master of the kitchen, blending Brazilian and French culinary influences. $$$$

**Quadrifoglio**, Rua J.J. Seabra 19, tel: 294 1433. Sophisticated bistro with an interesting menu featuring a good selection of pastas. $$$

*Leblon*

*Bread baked hourly at Garcia & Rodrigues*

**Garcia & Rodrigues**, Avenida Ataulfo de Paiva 1251, tel: 512 8188. French deli with a restaurant and café. $$$$

**Antiquarius**, Rua Aristídes Espínola 19, tel: 294 1049. This fashionable restaurant is technically Portuguese, but the menu offers a wide range of interesting dishes. $$$

**Bibi Sucos**, Avenida Ataulfo de Paiva 591. Fruit juice. $

## Botequims

*Botequims* (small bar-restaurants) offer traditional snacks and meals at reasonable prices. All those listed have a good local atmosphere to go with the food.

*Botafogo and Flamengo*

**Aurora**, Rua Cap. Salomão 43. Founded in 1929. Popular with artists and journalists. Specialty: *lula com arroz* (octopus with rice). **Lamas**, Rua Marquês de Abrantes 18. Founded in 1874; one of the original bohemian bar-restaurants. Specialty: *canja de galinha* (chicken and rice).

### Centro

**Amarelinho**, Praça Floriano, Cinelândia. Great place to watch the world go by. Specialty: *frango à passarinho* (fried chicken pieces). **Arco do Teles**, Travessa do Comércio, Praça XV. The whole street is very popular in the evening, especially on Friday, with live music outside. Specialty: *sardinha frita* (fried sardines). **Bar Luiz**, Rua da Carioca 39. Traditional restaurant established in 1887. Restaurant seating with German food. Specialty: *salsichão com mostarda preta* (large sausage with black mustard). **Monteiro**, Rua da Quitanda 83. Opened in 1916, it has a famous painting of a priest drinking. Specialty: *sanduíche de pernil* (leg of pork sandwich). **Paladino**, Rua Uruguaiana 224. A piece of Rio's history since 1908, this is a food shop with huge displays, and a bar-restaurant. Specialty: *sanduíches de frios* (cold sandwiches).

*Copacabana refreshment*

### Copacabana

**Adega Pérola**, Rua Siqueira Campos 138. Seventy types of hot food. Specialty: *batatinha à lagareira* potatoes. **Cervantes**, Rua Barata Ribeiro 7. Specialty: *filé mignon* with cheese and pineapple sandwich.

### Ilha da Mandala

**Ilha da Mandala** Tiny, exclusive island restaurant accessible only by boat (contact Igor and Marcia Babolin mobile tel: 9187 5751 or VHF canal 10 ship-to-shore radio). Specializes in sushi, seafood and barbecued palmito. With a nightclub, a favorite haunt of Brazil's footballers. $$$$

*Sushi at Ihla da Mandala*

### Ipanema

**Bofetada**, Rua Frame de Amode 87. Specialty: *romário x túlio* (beans and meat stew).

### Lapa

**Casa da Cachaça**, Avenida Mem de Sá 110. Specializing in Brazilian *pinga* made from sugar cane, as well as sardines followed by *cachaça*. **Bar Brasil**, Avenida Mem de Sá 90. Founded in 1907. German food. Specialty: *Eisbein com chucrute* (pork knuckle with sauerkraut).

### Leblon

**Bracarense**, Rua José Linhares 85. Specialty: *bolinho de aipim com camarão* (cassava and prawns). **Flor do Leblon**, Rua Dias Ferreira 52. Specialty: *picanha* (barbecued beef). **Jobi**, Avenida Ataulfo Paiva 1166. Seating inside or out. Specialty: *caldinho de feijão* (bean stew).

### Santa Teresa

**Sobrenatural**, Rua Alm. Alexandrino 423 (Lgo. Guimarães). Informal and popular with samba musicians.

# Nightlife

When the sun goes down Rio gets ready to party, with hundreds of bars and clubs that do not close until well into the early hours. Shows at the famous **Plataforma Showhouse** take the visitor through Rio's cultural past with a mixture of music, carnival and exotic dances. The classical arts also have a home in the city's **Teatro Municipal** where opera, ballet and classical music are presented on a regular basis. There are also theaters and cinemas showing the latest plays and films (sub-titled).

Discos and nightclubs in Rio suddenly become the in place and just as suddenly close down or change name and theme. So do confirm details of venues with staff at your hotel or check in the local newspapers. Those listed below are well established.

*Stepping out at Sol e Mar*

*Samba at The Ballroom*

### Dancing

**Bar 121**, Rio-Sheraton Hotel, Avenida Niemeyer 121, Vidigal, tel: 274 1122. Cheek-to-cheek dancing for all ages in grand hotel luxury.

**Fun Club**, 4th floor, Shopping Rio Sul, tel: 541 1478. Disco for teenage and young people. Excellent security. Bar with food. Gets busy from 10pm.

**Sol e Mar**, Avenida Repórter Nestor Moreira 11, tel: 543 1663. Formal ballroom dancing for the more mature dancer with live bands and popular records. Excellent restaurant attached (*see page 78*).

**The Ballroom**, Rua Humaitá 110, Botafogo, tel: 537 7600. Live music with Brazilian popular bands. *Bossa nova*, samba, *forró* and *maracatú* rhythms and country rock are regular sounds. All ages. Formal dancing and freestyle as well on a huge dance floor. Bar and restaurant.

### Shows

**Canecão**, Avenida Venceslau Brás 215, Botafogo, tel: 543 1241.

**Metropolitan**, Shopping Via Parque, Avenida Ayrton Senna 3000, Barra da Tijuca, tel: 421 1331.

**Mistura Fina**, Avenida Borges de Medeiros 3207, Lagoa, tel: 537 2844.

*The exotic Plataforma*

**Plataforma**, Rua Adalberto Ferreira, 32-Leblon, tel: 274 4022. The tourist show depicting quintessential Rio through music and exotic dance.

### Theaters

**Carlos Gomes**, Rua Pedro 1 22, Centro, tel: 232 8701.

**João Caetano**, Praça Tiradentes, Centro, tel: 221 0305.

**Nelson Rodrigues**, Avenida República do Chile 230, Centro, tel: 262 0942.

**Teatro Municipal**, Praça Floriano, Centro, tel: 297 4411.

## Shopping

*Summer collection in Centro*

The shopping habits of the Cariocas changed at the start of the 1980s with the opening of the first of the city's giant shopping malls, **Shopping Rio Sul** (Rua Lauro Muller 116, Botafogo, tel: 545 7200. Monday to Saturday 10am–10pm, Sunday 10am–6pm. Free transfer bus from Metro Cardeal Arcoverde in Copacabana every 30 minutes).

**83**

Prior to the opening of the climatically controlled centers, residents shopped in the day when the temperatures in the streets of Copacabana and Ipanema began to fall. **Ipanema** (based around Rua Visconde de Pirajá), and the city center during the working week, still have their fans, but for the vast majority of shoppers the choice is the large centers which offer hundreds of stores as well as supporting departments stores, restaurants, bars and even cinemas and theaters.

*Ipanema elegance*

Rio Sul was followed in 1981 by **Barra Shopping** (Avenida das Américas 4666, Barra da Tijuca, tel: 431 9922. Monday to Saturday 10am–10pm, Sunday 10am–9pm). By 1994 this had grown to become Latin America's largest shopping complex. With its own fully equipped medical center and monorail service, Barra Shopping is more like a small town. At last count, it had 554 shops selling just about everything imaginable; 10 cinemas; a theater; an amusement park; bowling alley; and 42 restaurants. The Praça XV Market Place, on the lower floor, has attractive displays of a wide range of food.

*Barra Shopping*

Other popular shopping centers include **Fashion Mall** (Auto Estrada Lagoa-Barra 899, São Conrado); **Downtown** ( (Avenida das Américas, Barra da Tijuca); and **Via Parque** (Avenida Ayrton Senna 3000, Barra da Tijuca). There is also **Shopping Casino Atlântico** (Avenida Atlântica 4240, Copacabana) specializing in antiques and art galleries.

# Getting There

*Opposite: downtown directions*

## By air

Rio is connected to the world by most of the major European, US and Asian airlines, many of which have daily services that land in São Paulo as well. The city is also served by the Brazilian carriers, including Varig (Avenida Rio Branco, 227G, Centro, tel: 220 3821); VASP (Rua Santa Luzia 735, Centro: tel: 0800 998277); Transbrasil (Rua Santa Luzia 651, Centro, tel: 297 4422) and Tam (Avenida Franklin Roosevelt 194, tel: 0800 123100).

*Aeroporto Santos Dumont*

International flights and most domestic services arrive at Galeão Aeroporto Internacional do Rio de Janeiro (Ilha do Governador, Av 20 de Janeiro, tel: 021 398 6060. Flight information, tel: 398 4526, 398 4527). Riotur, the city tourist board, has a desk in the arrivals terminal with English-speaking staff.

Taxi fares are about R$50,00 to the main hotel areas, and about R$15,00 to Zona Sul. Several companies have booths inside the airport terminal for the pre-payment of fares, which is usually cheaper than by the meter, and most take credit cards. All the companies accept credit cards if you pay within the taxi.

85

A cheaper option is the executive bus operated by Real Express (5.20am–midnight, about every 20 minutes, R$7,00). One bus goes to the airport of Santos Dumont, in the downtown area, the other via much of the Centro area to the Zona Sul, and passes all the major hotels. The bus stop is the other side of the metal fence by the taxi rank. Tell the driver where you want to get off.

Alternatively, the Rio-São Paulo Shuttle uses Aeroporto Santos Dumont (Praça Senador Salgado Filho, Centro, tel: 524 7070. Flight information, tel: 0800 24 4646). Executive buses go to Zona Sul from here.

*Real buses leave every 20 minutes*

## By sea

There is no regular boat service to Brazil. Major cruise companies such as Oremar and Linea C run trips along the Atlantic coast of South America during the European winter, and several round-the-world cruises stop off at Rio. Some offer special Carnival trips.

## By bus and coach

There are bus services between Rio and major cities in neighboring South American countries, with direct lines to Asuncion (Paraguay), Buenos Aires (Argentina), Montevideo (Uruguay) and Santiago (Chile). Though an excellent way to explore the country, services are slow, hot and distances very long, so flying is usually a better option. One of the major operators is Rodoviária Novo, Rio, tel: 021 291 5151.

*All aboard for Leblon*

*Metro logo*

*A yellow Taxi Comum*

# Getting Around

## Local buses

In the Zona Sul area most buses are new, clean and generally safe. Get on at the back, pay the conductor, pass through the turnstile, and get off at the front. The drivers, along with local police, have been instructed in how to help tourists who don't speak much Portuguese.

## Metro

The two underground lines extend from downtown Rio north to the suburb of Irajá and south to Botafogo. The metro is clean and safe and the fastest way to get from Copacabana to the city center. There is just one price (R$1,00) for a single ticket, whatever distance you go and even if you transfer from one line to the other. Linha 1: 6am–11pm, Linha 2: 5.30am–11pm, closed Sunday.

## Taxis

There are various taxis that wait at stands or have radios, but the only ones that are allowed to be hailed in the street are the yellow Taxi Comum, which have an illuminated 'Taxi' sign on top.

Taxis drivers should clearly display their official photo identification badge issued by the local council, and have a meter. The meter has two tariffs; Tariff 2 is from 9pm to 6am and all day Sunday and holidays, and is 20 percent more than Tariff 1. Refuse a flat fare without the meter because it will cost at least double. Baggage in the boot costs R$0,70 per piece.

Taxis in Rio are cheaper than other international cities, but drivers are not required to pass any test of knowledge of Rio's streets so may not know their way around and have to use a map. The Radio Taxis cost about 30 percent more than the Taxi Comum, but are larger and air-conditioned. The drivers are also more knowledgeable.

## Car hire

A major credit card, passport and international driving licence are required to hire a car. All the main international car hire companies have desks at the airports, but most also have depots in Avenida Princesa Isabel in Copacabana. Some companies do not offer full insurance for damage or theft, unless asked for. It is advisable to have it to avoid being left with a huge bill if the car is damaged or stolen. In all cases of loss or damage the company will require a police report for the insurance claim.

Major car hire companies in close proximity in Avenida Princesa Isabel include: Avis, tel/fax: 295 7340: Localiza, tel: 275 3340; Locanit, tel: 543 1125 or 275 4448; and Unidas, tel: 275 8299 or 0800 121 121.

## Facts for the Visitor

*Visitors to Quinta Boa Vista*

### Visas

EU citizens do not need a visa, but US, Canadian and Australians should apply for visas, which last three months, at their Brazilian consulate. On arrival immigration officials will stamp your arrival/departure card. This must be kept safe as you need to return it on departure. Failure to do so results in lengthy delays and a possible fine.

Identification must by law be carried at all times in Brazil. Fortunately the police do not enforce this at the beach, and, if you are worried about carrying a passport around, a copy will be accepted. Find a *cartes o* (photocopy shop) which are licenced to make certified copies.

*Information is also available from machines*

### Tourist information

**In the UK:** Rio Tour, 421a Finchley Road, London NW3 6HJ (tel: 020-7431 0303, fax: 020-7431 7920, website: www.rio.rj.gov.br/riotour).
**In the US:** Brazilian Embassy, 3006 Massachusetts Avenue, Washington DC 20008–3699 (tel: 202-238 2700).
**In Rio:** Embratur (Brazilian Tourism Authority), Rua Mariz e Barros 13, Praça da Bandeira (tel: 273 2212, fax: 273 9290). There is also a Tourist Information Centre at the same address (tel: 273 1516, 293 1313 ext 2112/2119). TurisRio (Rio de Janeiro State Tourist Board), Rua da Assembléia 10 (tel: 531-1922, fax: 531-2506). Riotur (City of Rio de Janeiro Tourism Authority) operates from the same address (tel: 217 7575, fax: 531 1872).
Rio Convention & Visitors' Bureau, Rua Visconde de Pirajá , 547, Ipanema, tel: 259 6165, fax: 511 2592.

*The national bank*

### Money

The Brazilian currency is the Real (plural is Reis), with 100 centavos in 1 Real. Notes come in denominations of

*Visa cards are accepted here*

1, 5, 10, 50 and 100 Reis, and coins in 1, 5, 10, 25, 50 centavos and 1 Real. Avoid 100 and 50 Reis notes as it is often very difficult to change large denomination notes, even in banks.

Most large hotels change money and travelers' checks, but offer a poor rate. There are a numbers of *casa de câmbio* money-changing agents that offer better rates, in Avenida Nossa Senhora de Copacabana and Avenida Rio Branco. US dollars or sterling are preferred. Money is available from ATM machines. Banco do Brasil and Bradesco accept Visa cards; Banco 24 Horas American Express; and the Citybank service at some Blockbuster video shops accepts most cards including MasterCard.

Hotels and restaurants accept credit cards, but some of the better-known ones surprisingly do not. People pay by check.

### Voltage
Rio's is 110 volts (60 cycles) but many hotels offer 220 volts as well. Not all of Brazil is 110 volts, however.

### Time
Most of Brazil, including Rio, is three hours behind GMT. Since 1985, Brazil has introduced daylight-saving time in summer. It normally goes into effect in October (clocks forward) and ends in February which means the time difference between Rio and London, for example, can swing between two and four hours.

*Direct dial*

### Telephones
Public phones in Brazil use either tokens or phonecards, which can be obtained at news-stands, bars or shops. Also called an *orelhão* (big ear) because of the protective shell surrounding it, the yellow telephone is for local or collect calls, and blue for direct-dial long-distance calls within the country. Neither operates calls to other countries.

For international calls you need to use a phone in a hotel or *posto telefônico* (telephone company station) at most bus stations and airports. International calls placed through the Brazilian state telephone company Embratel are very expensive. It is better to go through one of the discount companies such as AT&T, Cable & Wireless Téléconnect, and so on, with a calling card.

The international code for Brazil is: 55.
The city code for Rio de Janeiro is: 021.

### Postal services
The opening times of the post offices (*correios*) vary but are usually Monday through Friday 8am–6pm and until noon on Saturday. The only post office open 24 hours a day is at the international airport.

## Telecommunications

Telegrams can be sent from any post office, or phone 135 (national) or 000222 (international). Alternatively, your hotel can arrange this for you.

Faxes can be sent from most hotels and any post office, or there are many office services bureaux, travel agents and other outlets offering faxing services. Check on costs, however, as charges can vary enormously.

## Opening times

**Banks**: Monday to Friday 10am–4.30pm.
**Gas stations**: allowed to operate 24 hours a day, although not all do.
**Offices**: Monday to Friday 9am–6 pm.
**Shopping centers**: Monday to Saturday 10am–10pm. Some malls open on Sunday and those stores that do then only open at 1pm or later on Monday.
**Shops**: Monday to Saturday 9am–6.30pm or later.

## Public holidays

1 January: New Year's Day
20 January: St Sebastian's Day, the patron saint of Rio de Janeiro
February/March: Carnival (starts on the Friday before Lent and ends on Ash Wednesday)
March/April: Good Friday
21 April: Tiradentes Day
1 May: Labor Day
May/June: Corpus Christi
7 September: Independence Day
12 October: Nossa Senhora da Aparecida (Brazil's national Saint's day)
2 November: All Souls' Day
15 November: Republic Day
25 December: Christmas Day

*Ballet on St Sebastian's Day*

## Carnival tips

It is not difficult for the visitor to enjoy Carnival. Most hotels and travel agents can arrange tickets to the balls and seats for main parades, and the more time you give them, the better the prices and seats will be. The top schools traditionally parade on Sunday and Monday night, starting at around 7pm and going on through until 5am or later. The most comfortable way to see the parade is from a box (*camarote*), but these cost thousands of dollars per head and the majority are paid for by big companies or very rich individuals. A better option is the *cadeiras de pista* and *frisas*, the ringside seats that consist of a table and four chairs or a box area for six. These will cost US$150–500 per person depending on their location. It is also possible for visitors actually to join in with a school,

*Carnival in progress*

but this needs to be arranged in advance through the hotel or local residents who have contacts at the samba schools.

Tourists should not worry unduly about crime during Carnival because the vast majority of the crime is drug related or happens in areas where visitors would not venture. However, take care when crossing any road or driving, as motor accident statistics are still frighteningly high during the celebrations.

## Sightseeing tours

### Cultural tour

A mini-bus tour around the Centro district offering good value for people in a hurry. Leaves once an hour from Paço Imperial (11.30am–7.30pm). The price does not include museum admissions.

*Dressed for the ball*

### Carlos Roquette

Carlos Roquette has been leading tours in Rio since 1983, including an historical downtown, architectural and rare-bookshop tour. He also runs an 'at your own risk' tour of Rio's seedier night spots and a 'lonesome, single, divorced' over-40s tour. He is a mine of information about the latest, and safest, places to go clubbing. Prices vary according to the tour (tel: 322 4872, fax: 547 4774).

### Favela tour

Run by Marcelo Armstrong, the tour takes in Favela Rocinha, the largest *favela* (shanty town) in Brazil, and the Vila Canoas where community projects and the local people make visitors welcome (daily; tel: 322 2727, mobile: 9989 0074).

*Staying in lane*

### Atlantic Forest jeep tour

Covering the Parque Nacional da Tijuca and trails using World War II jeeps, the tour explores the natural beauty of the world's biggest urban forest. (daily US$35,00; tel: 511 2220). The Parque Nacional da Tijuca is also popular with cyclists and walkers. However, it is the largest urban forest in the world and it is very easy to get lost off the beaten track, but with a guide the forest is one of the great experiences of Rio. Guides include Carlos Millan, tel: 522 5586 or 9966 7010; ecology tour, tel/fax: 522 1620.

## Active pursuits

### Cycling/skating

A 16-km (10-mile) cycle and skate lane runs from the far end of Leblon Beach along the seafront at Ipanema and Copacabana, down Avenida Princesa Isabel, into Botafogo and along Flamengo Park. Bikes and skates can be rented at a number of locations along the route, including Stop Bike, Rua Barata Ribeiro, 181, Galeria Gam James, loja

L, tel: 275 7345 (directly opposite Metro Cardeal Arcoverde, Copacabana). It is also possible to cycle and skate around the Lagoa (*see page 35*).

*Diving*

The best places for diving are either Búzios or Angra dos Reis. Because Rio's beaches have strong surf and the shoreline drops away suddenly, novice swimmers should be careful, but in Búzios and Angra the waters are sheltered and clear. The strong surf also means that jet ski activity is restricted in Rio to the Marapendi Canal. Try Jet Club, Estrada da Barra da Tijuca 465, Canal de Marapendi (tel: 493 4180). Clube do Jet-PJ, Estrada da Barra da Tijuca 433 (tel: 494 3833).

*Golf*

Golf is not a major sport with the resident population and the city has only two full courses, both private clubs. These do let visitors play in the week but you should call in advance. The clubs are the Gávea Golf Club (Estrada da Gávea 800, São Conrado; tel: 322 4141) and the Itanhangá Golf and Country Club (Estrada da Barra 2005, Barra; tel: 494 2507). Open to the public is the six hole, par-3 Golden Green (Posto 7, Praia da Barra; tel: 433 3950).

*Hang-gliding*

Recommended pilots include Carlos Millan (tel: 522 5586 or 9966 7010), Rui Mara (tel: 9982 5703), Alex Rezende (tel: 322 0730), Edivaldo Ferreira (tel: 9988 5821), Alex Brasil (tel: 273 9733), Paulo Cesar (tel: 9984 5643) and Paulo Selan (tel: 595 1835). Brazil's Hang-gliding Association, Praia do Pepino, São Conrado (tel/fax: 322 0266) operates the landing point at Praia do Pepino Beach.

## On the streets

Businessmen wear smart tropical business suits, but otherwise the general look is casual, and T-shirt and shorts are acceptable in most places except government buildings. Don't wear expensive jewelry or watches when walking around, however.

Be careful when crossing the road, particularly at night when many drivers don't bother to stop at red lights, even if pedestrians have right of way. Drivers in Rio don't respect pedestrians and expect people to get out of their way when they suddenly emerge from underground car parks.

The local council now asks tourists not to buy anything from street kids. These children are probably controlled by adults and over the past few years the council has made a valiant effort to rehabilitate them into projects where they can be looked after properly.

## Crime

The mayor's office has made a big effort to beat crime over the past few years and Rio's tourist police say that the

*Diving at Búzios*

*Swimming at Angra*

91

*Landing at Pepino Beach*

violent crime statistics are considerably reduced. However, they also report that tourists have been using Rio's past reputation to make false claims from insurance companies, and this is now under investigation by Interpol.

Places that tourists have heard of – Copacabana, Ipanema and Leblon – are all in the Zona Sul area, and it is unlikely that a visitor will have any trouble there whatsoever. During the day the police presence is heavy, and many shops and hotels employ private security guards. Visitors should be careful, as in any big city, with personal belongings and security, however.

At night there are two places to be avoided: the red light area of Copacabana (Avenida Atlântica from the Copacabana Palace Hotel to Avenida Princesa Isabel, extending to a few blocks inland and including Praça do Lido), and the red-light district in Lapa (around Avenida Mem de Sá). At all times of day it is inadvisable to walk through any of the tunnels connecting the different areas.

*Tourists can feel safe in the Zona Sul*

## Emergencies

**Rio Tourist Police** (24-hour specialist service for tourists, opposite Scala nightclub), Avenida Afrânio de Melo Franco, Leblon (tel: 690 3590 or 690 3591, fax: 690 3598 or 690 3593).
**Police** (Polícia Militar), tel: 190.
**First aid** (Pronto Socorro), tel: 192.
**Fire Brigade** (Corpo de Bombeiros), tel: 193.

## Medical services

**24-hour medical clinics**: Galdino Campos Cárdio Copa, Avenida Nossa Senhora de Copacabana 492 (tel: 548 9966 or 548 3530). Cárdio Plus, Rua Visconde de Pirajá 330, Ipanema (tel: 521 4899).
**24-hour dentist**: Policlínica Barata Ribeiro, Rua Barata Ribeiro 51, Copacabana, tel: 275 4697 or 275 4133.
**24-hour pharmacies**: Drogaria Pacheco are at the following places: Avenida Nossa Senhora de Copacabana 115A (tel: 295 7555 or 295 5103); Avenida Nossa Senhora de Copacabana 543A/B (tel: 548 1525 or 548 3166); Rua do Catete 248, Catete (tel: 556 6792 or 558 3389); Rua Voluntários da Pátria 357A, Botafogo (tel: 266 4035); Rua Olegário Macial 520, Barra (tel: 493 3300); Farmácia do Leme, Avenida Prado Junior 237, Leme (tel: 275 3848); City Farma, Rua Humaitá 95A, Humaitá (tel: 266 6060).

## Toilets

Toilets in bus stations cost about R$1,00, and there are facilities inside most long-distance buses. At the beach the lifeguard stations along the front have public toilets, showers and nappy-changing facilities. Locals tend to use the toilets in restaurants and bars.

*Always on hand*

*Copacabana Palace Hotel*

# Accommodations

There is a wide choice of accommodations in Rio to suit every taste and budget and, as it is fairly easy to get around the city from the Zona Sul, location is not as important as it might seem. Traditionalists will head for Copacabana, which has easy access to the city center and major attractions and offers a wide selection of hotels from the palatial Copacabana Palace to the simpler two- and three-star hotels in the back streets. Visitors looking to spend more time soaking up the sun than sightseeing may prefer the resort hotels like the Sheraton and Inter-Continental.

When booking, always ask if there is a promotion or discount available (hotel rates can drop dramatically out of season if you are staying for more than one night), or indicate you have found somewhere else less expensive with better facilities. Many offers are on the Internet.

For longer rents Rio has inexpensive *apart-hotels* in the Zona Sul area which offer hotel service but are privately owned apartments available to rent for a month or more. Check any of the local newspapers for advertisements.

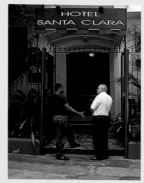

*The Santa Clara, a quiet, family-run hotel*

## Accommodations in the Zona Sul area

Prices are for a standard double room including breakfast: $=up to R$60, $$=up to R$120, $$$=up to R$200, $$$$=above R$200.

### Botafogo and Flamengo

**Florida Hotel**, Rua Ferreira Viana 81, Flamengo; tel: 556 5242, fax: 285 5777. This is a modern hotel but with lots of traditional style. It offers a rooftop pool, plus good food. All cards. $$$

**Flamengo Palace Hotel**, Rua Corrêa Dutra 31, Flamengo; tel: 556 5343. A nicely appointed modern hotel in a side street just walking distance from the beautiful Parque do

*Breakfast at the Sofitel*
*Rio Palace*

*The elegant Miramar Palace*

Flamengo, and very close to Metro Catete. All cards. $$
**Albergue Chave**, Rua General Dionísio 63, Botafogo; tel: 286 0303, fax: 286 5652. Rio's official youth hostel offers excellent value for the budget traveler. No cards. $

*Copacabana*
**Copacabana Palace**, Avenida Atlântica 1702, Copacabana; tel: 548 7070, fax: 235 7330. This is the most famous hotel in Brazil, if not South America. Inaugurated in 1923, it has been completely refurbished since being taken over by Orient-Express Hotels in 1989. Among many luxury attractions, it offers the best and most stylish hotel pool in Rio, and is the site of one of the main Carnival and New Year balls. All cards. $$$$
**Sofitel Rio Palace**, Avenida Atlântica 4240, Copacabana; tel: 525 1232, fax: 525 1200. Recent addition to the international Sofitel group, this hotel is at the far end of the beach and has great views from the rooms and the pool terrace. There is first-class service and excellent restaurants. All cards. $$$$
**Méridien Copacabana** , Avenida Atlântica 1020, Copacabana; tel: 546 0880, fax: 541 6447. Rising 37 floors above the beach, the Méridien offers breathtaking views over the beach from most of its rooms. It is particularly popular with French and Italian visitors, and the rooftop restaurant, Le Saint Honoré, is one of the city's best. All cards. $$$$
**Rio Othon Palace**, Avenida Atlântica 1500, Copacabana, tel: 522 1522, fax: 522 1697. A first-class hotel and one of the landmarks halfway along the beach. A small rooftop pool, and several restaurants. All cards. $$$$
**Miramar Palace Hotel**, Avenida Atlântica 3668, Copacabana, tel: 521 1122, fax: 521 3294. A traditional and elegant hotel with many rooms overlooking the beach. Good restaurant and service. All cards. $$$
**Majestic Rio Palace Hotel**, Rua Cinco de Julho 195, Copacabana, tel: 255 2030, fax: 255 1692. With 82 rooms and two suites, sauna, swimming pool, restaurant and conference facilities, this offers everything you would expect from a first-class hotel, but at a reasonable price. It is located in a quiet street, five minutes' walk from the beach. All cards. $$
**Santa Clara**, Rua Décio Vilares 316, Copacabana, tel: 256 2650, fax: 547 4042. Run by Sr. Heber Brandão and family, this quiet little hotel has individual rooms and a nice atmosphere. Air-conditioning but no credit cards. $
**Copacabana Praia**, Rua Tenente Marones de Gusmão 85, Copacabana; tel: 547 5422, fax: 235 3817. With 51 apartments, this used to be a youth hostel, but now offers excellent value for singles, doubles and larger groups, although it does not have air-conditioning. It is located

in a very quiet area, 10 minutes' walk from the beach. All cards. $

### Glória and Centro
**Hotel Glória**, Rua do Russel 632, Glória; tel: 555 7272, fax: 555 7282. A small piece of Brazilian history. Stacked with works of art. Individually appointed rooms. Great view from the pool. Family-run with enthusiastic staff. All cards. $$$$
**Guanabara Palace Hotel**, Avenida Presidente Vargas 392, Centro; tel: 253 8622, fax: 516 1582. Large downtown hotel convenient for the historic center. Rooftop pool with great view of the bay and Centro area. All cards. $$

### Ipanema and Leblon
**Caesar Park**, Avenida Vieira Souto 460, Ipanema; tel: 525 2525, fax: 521 6000. A really superb five-star hotel and a favorite with many celebrities. Rooftop pool, magnificent food and service in a great location. All cards. $$$$
**Marina Palace**, Avenida Delfim Moreira 630, Leblon; tel: 259 5212, fax: 274 5641. A nicely appointed hotel on the front with rooms at a reasonable price for the area. All cards. $$$

### São Conrado and Vidigal
**Inter-Continental**, Avenida Prof. Mendes de Morais 222, São Conrado; tel: 322 2200, fax: 322 5500. All cards. $$$$
**Rio Sheraton Rio Hotel & Towers**, Avenida Niemeyer 121, Vidigal; tel: 274 1122, fax: 239 5643. All cards. $$$$
Both of these hotels are top international resort properties with a fine selection of restaurants and bars, tennis courts and substantial pool areas. Popular with executives looking for high standards with a tropical, relaxing flavor.

*Marina Palace*

*Rooftop pool at the Caesar Park*

# Index